STRESS
IN POLICING

STRESS IN POLICING

HANS TOCH

With contributions by
Frankie Y. Bailey and Marty Floss

AMERICAN PSYCHOLOGICAL ASSOCIATION
WASHINGTON, DC

Published by
American Psychological Association
750 First Street, NE
Washington, DC 20002
www.apa.org

To order	Tel: (800) 374-2721, Direct: (202) 336-5510
APA Order Department	Fax: (202) 336-5502, TDD/TTY: (202) 336-6123
P.O. Box 92984	Online: www.apa.org/books/
Washington, DC 20090-2984	Email: order@apa.org

In the U.K., Europe, Africa, and the Middle East, copies may be ordered from
American Psychological Association
3 Henrietta Street
Covent Garden, London
WC2E 8LU England

Typeset in Palatino by EPS Group Inc., Easton, MD

Printer: United Book Press, Inc., Baltimore, MD
Cover designer: NiDesign, Baltimore, MD
Technical/Production Editor: Jennifer Powers

The opinions and statements published are the responsibility of the authors, and such opinions and statements do not necessarily represent the policies of the American Psychological Association.

Library of Congress Cataloging-in-Publication Data
Toch, Hans.
   Stress in policing / Hans Toch with contributions by Frankie Bailey and Marty Floss.—1st ed.
      p. cm.
   Includes bibliographical references and index.
   ISBN 1-55798-829-3 (alk. paper)
      1. Police—Job stress—United States.   2. Police administration—United States.   3. Police subculture—United States.   4. Police—United States—Attitudes.   5. Occupational surveys—United States.
I. Bailey, Frankie Y.   II. Floss, Marty.   III. Title.

HV7936.J63 T63 2001
363.2'01'9—dc21

2001046460

British Library Cataloguing-in-Publication Data
A CIP record is available from the British Library.

Printed in the United States of America
First Edition

To the memory of J. Douglas Grant,
a great colleague and a good friend.

Contents

Foreword

Chief Gil Kerlikowske
Seattle Police Department

Law enforcement in modern America is producing new challenges for both the leaders of police organizations and those who patrol the streets. These challenges are increasingly complex and appearing with unprecedented rapidity. Police leaders are constantly given the charge by elected officials, the media, employee organizations, and the public for clear and specific direction. Yet we are a part of a society that is continually changing and ever ambiguous.

Hans Toch has taken on a subject of immense importance, not only to those engaged in the profession of law enforcement, but also to the citizens we serve who want and need to trust the institution of policing and the people who protect them day in and day out. In my opinion, his most significant contribution through this book is highlighting the importance of "bottom-up," or employee-driven, workplace change.

Professor Toch is highly regarded for his academic work in problem-solving, use of force, and stress. But to the practitioners in the world of policing he is respected for a trait beyond academia: He cares deeply and passionately about our calling and the people who have answered that call. *Stress in Policing* provides researchers and practitioners alike with a rich and meaningful understanding of just what is affecting our local law enforcement organizations. This text is both a wake-up call and a warning for elected officials, law enforcement leaders, and anyone who cares about how their cities and towns are policed.

This wake-up call stresses the importance of improving law enforcement, not just in areas of efficiency and effectiveness, but also in how the organization cares for and respects its people. The warning heralds the importance that creating and maintaining high-quality police departments is the responsibility of not only of enforcement executives, but of every stakeholder who benefits from or uses this service.

One of the most significant contributions of this book is that it opens the inclusive and somewhat secretive day-to-day world of the police officer. Those who practice policing and those who study it are intimately familiar with what officers deal with as they respond to the calls and needs emanating from the public. Yet rarely do citizens, reporters, and those elected officials who oversee police departments have, or take, the opportunity to learn about what a police officer sees, feels, and experiences. Professor Toch is to be commended for inserting many of the detailed comments he has obtained from working officers. These enlightening and emotional comments force the reader into the world of policing, one fraught not only with the stress related to dangerous calls or terrible tragedies, but also with the stress of politics and administrations and the interpersonal conflicts that exist inside the locker room or police car.

Stress in Policing could not appear at a more appropriate time. As police departments attempt to deal with the concerns that have been raised over issues of racial profiling, increased citizen review regarding discipline, and how complaints against the police are dealt with, this book clearly illuminates the human side of policing. For after all of the analysis and study, that really is one of the basic missions of local law enforcement—the individual service to people.

Finally, Professor Toch's research squarely faces the difficult issue of race relations in today's law enforcement organizations. It provides a linchpin for those departments that wish to better understand and communicate about one of the most important issues affecting police departments.

The process of using employee-driven methods to improve the organization's response to complex issues involving fairness and equity is a hallmark of *Stress in Policing*. Everyone who has a vested interest in seeing their local law enforcement agency provide service in a principled and professional way will benefit from reading this book.

Preface

Around Easter of 1983 I was drafted as keynote speaker for a conference called "Stress and Violence in Criminal Justice." I cannot remember what I said there, but I have somehow rescued three vignettes that I used in my presentation.

One item related to an air traffic controller and his family. At this period of time, controllers had appointed themselves "poster boys" for occupational stress, and they were reaping a harvest of more or less favorable publicity. One newspaper story had attracted my attention. It featured an interview with the wife of a controller, who said that her husband persisted in directing traffic while at home. She specifically complained that "he sometimes orders us around like he is ordering planes to land." The wife also reported (with serendipitously felicitous wit) that it was hard for her spouse to "come down" after he arrived home. The husband acknowledged with appreciation his family's forbearance and understanding. He said that he recognized the problems he was unwittingly creating but concluded that understanding the effects of stress (which he said he did) was a far cry from being able to change one's behavior. He also said that because misery loved company, his group of controllers regularly met to reinforce each other's discontent.

My second vignette was a report I had read at the time covering a workshop on teacher stress and burnout. The report had focused on a study that purportedly showed that 20%–30% of teachers were vulnerable to burnout and that 10%–15% were already burned out. The data being cited, as it happened, supported no such conclusions. They suggested that most teachers loved their work and that they had other satisfying involvements. The highest ranked item in the study, in terms of intensity, was "I have been involved in outside activities which are as important to me as teaching." Almost next in line were "I have felt a total commitment to teaching," "I have felt exhilarated after working closely with my students," and "I have accomplished many worthwhile things on this job." The most frequently mentioned items showed the same combination of high-satisfaction themes (e.g., "I have felt I was positively influencing students' lives through my work" and "I have had time and energy for friends and family"). The alleged "burnout" items had been supplied by the researchers and thus of necessity had to appear in the rankings but did so in the lowest intensity, lowest frequency columns (New York State United Teachers, 1981).

The third illustration I invoked in my talk was a cautionary article written in 1980 by Suzanne Gordon, which contended that although "stress management [is] a lucrative new growth industry . . . the real cure to workplace stress may lie elsewhere." Gordon asked, Why might a worker be tense? She responded,

> It's obvious. Your superior has just ordered you to work overtime; management has been monitoring your telephone calls; you're trying to adjust to the new video display terminals the company has just installed to make processing information easier. Anyone working under these conditions is entitled to get uptight. (p. 39)

Gordon concluded that "programs on 'stress' seem unlikely to address the deeper causes of work tedium and powerlessness within the organizational hierarchy" (p. 40).

* * *

As I reappraise the odds and ends I accumulated two decades ago, I discover that they happily merge with my thinking today. I am forced to suspect that my own biases have not appreciably changed and that they may inform (or contaminate) the work that is reported in this book. It seems therefore appropriate for me to bring up one or two of my preconceptions.

I have long been concerned with occupational stress because I think the problem is important, but I have felt that the concept of "stress" has been frequently oversold. Some of my problems may have to do with the concept itself.

"Stress" is a transactional construct, which means that it refers to a process that links features of the human environment (stressors) with reactions to these features by people (stress-related behavior). But the sorts of links that are at issue are complex and difficult to pin down, which invites tenuous extrapolations.

The problem starts with the inception of the stress process. In theory, a stressor is as a stressor does. In other words, the stressor produces stress and is not a stressor if it does not produce stress. If I retain my equanimity while I am exposed to inhospitable circumstances, and subsequently am no worse for wear, I am presumptively not under stress. But I may come to see myself as an exception to a rule, as somehow coping with circumstances that overwhelm those made of less exceptional stuff.

I then may come to feel that I ought to be stressed, but somehow am not, and this situation is compounded when I am repeatedly told about my stressed colleagues, or my colleagues who are assumed to be stressed, and I find myself attending social conclaves (such as the convivial seminars of controllers or burnout workshops for teachers) in which stress for my occupation is defined as a normative response. Work environments such as mine can thus be stereotyped by their incumbents as stressful, even though more disadvantaged situations—like exploitive third world sweatshops and near-genocidal coal mines—might not be defined by their denizens as stressful.

Subjective definitions of what is stressful are, of course, one of the psychological links in the stress transaction and are a component of the stress concept. If one is affected by a stressor, one may be expected to become aware of the fact. One can similarly become aware of one's reaction to the experience. But one can be mistaken in one or another perception, especially if stress-related definitions happen to be more congenial, fashionable, or palatable than are alternative definitions, or more blatantly self-serving. The controller's wife may thus be according her "stressed" husband the undeserved benefit of a rationale for his habitually boorish dealings with his family.

Symptomatic behavior is more easily attributed to stress if an afflicted individual happens to be subjected to pressures or constraints at work. It may then be uninviting to postulate that the same person might manifest the same kinds of symptoms under more hospitable circumstances. An alcoholic who happens to have a difficult job is phenotypically indistinguishable from a worker whose drinking is a reaction to his situation and therefore a symptom of occupational stress. More seriously, if a person with clinical depression also has grounds for situational depression, one may blame his suicide on his job.

The converse also holds, as Gordon suggested. Pathogenic environments tend to intersect with vulnerabilities to their destructive effects, producing problems for people who would otherwise not experience them. Where such interactions occur, one cannot exonerate the custodians of the environment by pointing out that people who suffer its destructive impact are insufficiently resilient.

None of this should matter in practice, if one is in the business of ameliorating symptoms. Serious personal problems deserve to be attended to, irrespective of their origin or source. Therapeutic enterprises should never be so constituted that the stressed wheels get all the grease and that stress-unrelated symptoms come to invite less attention than do symptoms that are attributable to stress.

On the other hand, ameliorating symptoms—as Gordon noted—can itself be seen as an exonerating enterprise. Where authoritarian management styles or top-down organizational controls are sources of occupational stress, such conditions need to be targeted for change. But in this connection one can again argue that stress should not be the requisite or the criterion of intervention. Dysfunctional management practices need to be changed irrespective of whether they produce stress among workers who are exposed to destructive supervisory experiences. To wait for evidence of stress may needlessly delay essential organizational reform. This point has recently been illustrated in the U.S. Postal Service, where reforms were initiated after a series of incidents in which disgruntled employees reacted with (presumably stress-induced) violence.

A final problem that is produced for me by the concern with stress is one of potentially distorted perspective. There are many occupations, such as teaching and policing, that are exciting, fulfilling, actualizing, consuming, and enticing but may also be frustrating, taxing, and at times alienating or disillusioning. Such occupations are different from occupations that make unremitting demands in exchange for a compensatory paycheck. The latter sorts of occupations—such as routine assembly-line work—cry out for job redesign that can enrich the experience of the worker or for supportive counseling in the absence of enrichment.

An emphasis on stress obfuscates the difference between the two categories of occupations. This fact was vividly brought home to the air traffic controllers when they were fired by former President Ronald Reagan after overbidding their hands. Many of the unemployed controllers were forced to accept relatively menial employment. Interviews with such excontrollers were typically painfully suffused with nostalgia and redolent with golden memories of exciting days in the tower. There are obviously many professionals who do experience diminished work motivation at some points in their careers or cumulatively over time. Teachers take early retirement, guards end up in guard towers at the corner of prison walls, and some police count the days to their eligibility for pensions. Such workers resemble those in less challenging occupations and constitute an obvious problem for their employers. The differences between such workers and their colleagues need to be studied and attended to. Rekindling the motivation of burned-out professionals is also a challenge, as is the prevention of the corrosive development of burnout. On the other hand, where stress symptoms and burnout exist, it does not follow that they are symptomatic of problems posed for workers in an organization or that workers who burn out are representative of the work force. A balanced view of an occupation must encompass work motivation across the board to provide a context for the assessment of burnout and discontent.

* * *

Like other students of policing, I have read the literature that asserts that policing is a stressful occupation. However, most officers I have met in my own work seemed highly motivated (sometimes excessively so) and appeared to like their vocations. Admittedly, there were some men and women who did their share of grousing when an enticing opportunity afforded. I also remember officers who drank to excess, complained of paying multiple alimonies, or had occasional medical problems. One officer I worked with eventually retired on a disability at a relatively young age.

Although I cannot defend my experience as representative, I did not gain the impression that disproportionate numbers of officers could be categorized as stressed, in the technical meaning of the term. Insofar as I did see a problem, it was that any stressed police officer could be in a position to do serious harm. Police, after all, can use physical force and have the power to arrest people.

A more recent incentive for me to deal with police stress is the fact that stress-related interventions today are frequently innovative. I am especially impressed by efforts to prevent or reduce stress that are participatory in nature. My involvements with police have culminated in a set of officer-run performance review panels. In these groups, officers who had experienced physical conflicts with citizens worked with officers who appeared to be developing such problems. The success of this experience sold me on the power and promise of enterprises such as peer counseling and crisis intervention teams, which are nowadays the cutting edge of stress reduction experiments. I also became convinced that bottom-up change—irrespective of content area—is remarkably effective both in developing individuals and improving organizations.

Two specific developments made possible the work discussed in this book. The first was the fact that a person I considered a friend held a position of leadership in a police agency and manifested an interest in stress. The second was the timely availability of support for stress-related research.

I am indebted in this regard to the National Institute of Justice, although it should be obvious that neither the institute nor the departments in which our work was done bears responsibility for what follows. My opinions are very much my own, as are the errors and deficiencies of this book.

I am grateful to APA Books for serving as our publisher. This sponsorship is appropriate, given the seminal contribution of psychology in defining and responding to the police stress problem. Psychologists are responsible for the constructive focus on traumatic critical incidents. Psychologists also form the core of employee assistance programs and have earned enhanced credibility among police officers whom they assist. Psychologists have saliently responded to the needs and concerns of police family members. Much to their credit, they have also supported peer-counseling initiatives by providing training and showing hospitality to referrals. Last, as it has become painfully obvious that stress-related concerns of police officers are disproportionately organizational, psychologists have responded through organizational development consultation. I hope that some of the experiments in organizational development in which psychologists are involved will reach fruition. For it is the thesis of this book that no matter what else we may do to prevent and ameliorate stress, organizational change may hold the key to improving the lives of police officers.

Acknowledgments

I am in debt to the police departments that supported our work and to the officers who collaborated with us in our project. I shall be holding in remembrance their thoughtful collegiality and their valued contributions.

Because we advertised absolute confidentiality in our study, I cannot express my gratitude with the specificity our hosts deserve. Nor can I identify the two communities that extended their hospitality to us and provided the settings in which the officers worked.

The project outlined in this book was underwritten by the National Institute of Justice under Grant 96-IJ-CX-0056 ("Reduction of Stress Among Law Enforcement Officers and Their Families"), although opinions expressed in the book are those of the author and do not reflect views of the National Institute of Justice.

Among my benefactors at APA Books, I am beholden to Mary Lynn Skutley; to Judy Nemes, my redoubtable development editor; and to Jennie Reinhardt and Chris Davis. I am also grateful to an anonymous reviewer for constructive comments that provided unambiguous testimony to his identity.

Samuel Walker, Betsy Wright Kreisel, and Paula Kautt contributed to the work reported in the book. Jeannette Megas prepared the manuscript as usual. She has been known to correct my spelling but cannot be replaced by a computer.

STRESS IN POLICING

1

Introduction

"When constabulary duty's to be done," wrote Gilbert and Sullivan in 1880, "a policeman's lot is not a happy one." This tuneful dictum still strikes some observers as true. Such observers envisage policing as placing its incumbents at continuous risk. When they are not dodging bullets, officers are presumed to spend their time arresting resistant felons who must be wrestled to the ground. Also, the officers are conceived of running a steady gauntlet of taunting expletives from flagrantly ungrateful citizens.

No less an authority than Hans Selye—the man who single-handedly invented stress—once contended that policing is stressful. He wrote in 1978 that police work "ranks as one of the most hazardous [occupations], even exceeding the formidable stresses and strains of air traffic control" (p. 7). Other authorities have been equally assertive. Fennell (1981) rated policing as "the most dangerous job in the world emotionally" (p. 170). Axelbred and Valle (1978) concluded that "police work has been identified as the most psychologically dangerous job in the world" (p. 3). Somodeville (1978) proclaimed that "it is an accepted fact that a police officer is under stress and pressure unequalled by any other occupation" (p. 21).

The categorical contention that policing is outstandingly

stressful has come hand-in-hand with rosters of postulated stressors and lists of undesirable outcomes. Violence and danger on the job—or rather, the potential of violence and danger—has headed most lists of postulated stressors. Stimulus overload, stimulus underload, and (most plausibly) combinations of the two have been cited. Also high on most lists of stressors is the disruptive effect of shift work.

Studies that rely on officers themselves responding to survey questions yield a different picture. Such studies show that officers think of stressors as originating in the context of their work—especially, that of their superiors. As one officer observed, "the most stressful call is the one that summons you to headquarters." Brown and Campbell (1994) reported that

> When the police themselves were asked to list significant causes of stress they nominated the same occupational features which are associated with stress in the working lives of other kinds of employees. Officers from both the United States and the United Kingdom listed poor and insensitive supervision, unreasonable workload, shift work, personal safety and volume of paperwork as the most significant sources of stress at work. An authoritative British report suggested that stress could be mostly attributed to management and organizational factors. (p. 14)

Molloy and Mays (1984) concluded from their review of research studies that

> policing is probably stressful for reasons quite different from those typically presented in the literature. Judging from the strongest research in this area, it seems that helplessness and feelings of uncontrollability in the work environment may be a major source of stress for police officers. Beyond this, little can be safely concluded. (p. 207)

Kirschman (1997) has pointed out that most outside observers think of police as all-powerful, which in some senses they are. Yet officers "experience the terrible dilemma of being simultaneously powerful and powerless" (p. 55). When officers think of stress, they think of themselves as "constantly scrutinized, supervised, and reined in by their own department and by the community in ways that can be irritating, humiliating and sometimes irrelevant to their actual performance" (p. 55).

Ellison and Genz (1978, 1983) suggested that organizational stressors produce long-term chronic discontent but that acute discomfiting experiences (which most closely fit some technical definitions of stress) originate in discrete encounters, such as those involving serious cases of child abuse or the death of a fellow officer in the line of duty. Such encounters, which occur with varying frequency depending on the department and the officer's assignment, are sometimes referred to as "critical incidents" (see chapter 8). Lewis (1973) reported that in one municipal police department, officers averaged three injured adults a month, a life-threatening bleeding incident every three months, an injured child every two months, a victim of serious assault every two months, and a dead person every three months.

Sources of stress may thus vary depending on the sort of stress we refer to, and the same point may apply to consequences of stress. Organizational stressors may produce hostile reactions and alienation, while critical incidents may reinforce sleeping disorders or ulcers or undergird an officer's drinking problem.

Manifestations of Stress

Consequences of police stress that have been cited in the literature include those that are usually cited for other occupations, such as absenteeism and physical illness. But the most tangible police-related data point to slightly higher than expected mortality rates for illnesses ranging from coronary diseases to cancer (Violanti, Vena, & Petralia, 1998). In his review, Terry (1981) pointed out that despite such data, most police officers "consider themselves in good health and are satisfied with their state of health" (p. 66).

Beyond problems that may surface relating to officers' health and well-being, a variety of assorted consequences of police stress have been postulated. According to Terry (1981),

> Listed among these are divorce rates, marital discord, disruption of family life, child-rearing problems, sexual promiscuity, infidelity, jealousy, loss of nonpolice friends, alcoholism, suicide, police malpractice, "John Wayne Syndrome," overachievement, callousness, exploitiveness, high rates of performance anxieties, social anomie, polarization, and increasing citizen complaints and suits. (p. 67)

A more recent review (On-the-Job Stress in Policing, 2000) asserted that most "commonly reported" consequences of police stress include

- Cynicism and suspiciousness
- Emotional detachment from various aspects of daily life
- Reduced efficiency
- Absenteeism and early retirement
- Excessive aggressiveness (which may trigger an increase in citizen complaints)
- Alcoholism and other substance abuse problems
- Marital or other family problems (for example, extramarital affairs, divorce, or domestic violence)
- Post-traumatic stress disorder
- Heart attacks, ulcers, weight gain, and other health problems
- Suicide. (p. 20)

Divorce and suicide rates of police officers have been unfavorably compared with those of other occupations. Terry (1981) understatedly observed that "the list of persons who have commented upon the high divorce rates among officers is indeed long" (p. 67). However, despite the eloquent case that is often made for officers being in line for divorce because they are habitually unfaithful to their spouses or tend to treat their families like suspects, "the best available evidence supports the argument that police divorce rates are lower than the popular depiction of police family life would lead one to anticipate" (p. 68).

The relationship between job and family is also more intricate than is captured by the usual assertion that problems at work can spill over into family life. For one, problems at home can affect job performance. In the real world, moreover, no hard-and-fast line can be drawn through a person's feelings. To study the job/family stress area can become a daunting exercise in complexity. Fuller (1987) captured some of this complexity with a representative vignette:

> You are sitting in the squad room, the shift is over, and you have just arrested a suspect for domestic violence. The suspect is yelling and screaming and very difficult to deal with. He has brutally assaulted his wife, and she has been admitted to the hospital. The sight won't leave your mind for a long time. The Sergeant is demanding the end of your shift paperwork now! You pick up the phone and call your wife to tell her you will be late and will miss the kids' softball game. Your wife indicates that she is disgusted with your job. As you turn in your paperwork the Sergeant harps at you about the way you handled a call last week.
>
> As you drive home the picture of the domestic violence victim runs through your mind. You pull in your driveway, the house is dark, and you curse under your breath —another night staring at the TV. Your wife and kids are asleep, and there is nobody to talk to. You get a beer, sit down, and question why no one understands what you feel and realize how much you've changed over the years. You also realize how distant you have become from your family. The thought runs through your mind, "What do I do?" (p. 149)

The evidence does suggest that suicide rates among police officers may be higher than those for other occupations, although not every study on the subject documents this fact.[1] It is not obvious, moreover, that such differences can be traced to occupational stress. For example, few civilian workers who have become despondent are conveniently armed with loaded weapons on and off the job.[2] And it has also been found that police suicide rates vary widely, as do suicide rates generally. Even where suicide rates are highest, moreover, suicide remains a very low-frequency event. Low-frequency events generally are unlikely to result from across-the-board problems in an occupation or organization. No police stress reduction program would consider documenting its success with before-and-after inventories of officer suicide rates.

It goes without saying that most somatic or behavioral problems that people (including police officers) manifest are not the results of occupational stress. The fact that a person drinks excessively, suffers a heart condition, develops an ulcer, experiences frequent insomnia, or treats other people with disdain does not imply that his or her job is necessarily stressful, although a stress-related explanation may at times be inviting, reassuring, or remunerative.[3] By the same token,

---

[1]Stack and Kelley (1994) thus reported that when socioeconomic variables are controlled for, police no longer appear to have higher suicide rates than age-matched male peers. Andrews (1996), in Canada, found that most police suicides seemed to be motivated by concerns unrelated to work. Cases in which work stress was involved resembled those found for officers who did not commit suicide. Some officers who committed suicide, however, stood accused of illegal or unethical conduct.

[2]Members of the British Metropolitan Police force have traditionally not been issued firearms. Brown and Campbell (1994) pointed out that "male police officers in the United Kingdom have lower suicide rates than men in other occupational groups .... They have less than half the rate of judges, barristers or solicitors and are a quarter of the rate among dental practitioners" (p. 62). The Royal Ulster Constabulary in Northern Ireland, however, was routinely armed and had higher suicide rates than the general population from which the officers were drawn (p. 63).

[3]A recent New York Times story (Levy, 1999) alluded to a New York "heart bill" for correction officers extending benefits accorded to police officers 20 years earlier. The bill provides tax-free disability retirement pay to officers incurring heart conditions during their period of employment. The burden in this legislation is on the state to prove that a cardiac ailment is not occupationally stress related.

a person's work situation may be off-putting, frustrating, and annoying, without affecting the person adversely. People obviously differ in their reactions to problem situations. There are many individuals who are resilient and resourceful and have high levels of coping competence. Such people may not only deal effectively with untoward circumstances but may flourish under adversity.

Moreover, as the term *stress* has entered the general lexicon, it has obviously lost some of its pristine scientific connotations. We thus say that we are "stressed out" when we are tired or discouraged; we cite stress to justify moments of boorishness or shortness of temper. When we are invited to class circumstances we encounter in life as stressful or not stressful, we tend to call stressful any conditions that strike us as frustrating, annoying, or inconvenient.

Our propensity to equate stress with being frustrated— even where stress is meticulously defined in preambles to questionnaires—must be taken into account by researchers when they draw inferences from self-report studies. It means that the results of such studies at best are rosters of conditions nominated as *potential* stressors, because they are unpleasant, off-putting, or distasteful. Inventories of somatic symptoms and dysfunctional behavior also simply denote the *possibility* that stress may underlie the symptoms and behaviors at issue. This possibility obviously increases to the extent to which a roster of symptoms is more substantial than that obtained from comparison groups. The possibility also increases to the extent to which we find correlations between self-reported stress and symptomatology. In one recent study (National Institute of Justice, 1999), the researchers concluded, for example, that

> Officers reporting high stress (approximately 10 percent of all officers) were 3 times more likely to report poor health, 3 times more likely to abuse spouses or partners, 5 times more likely to report alcoholism, and 10 times more likely to experience depression than other officers. (p. 27)

Such findings are obviously not self-explanatory. They present us with chicken–egg issues because despondent officers may be more likely to define themselves as stressed, drink to excess, and endanger their health. Alcoholism, moreover, contributes to poor marital relations.

The Study of Stress

Most of what follows is drawn from a study conducted in two police departments in upstate New York. This study had several distinct features, some of which are more distinct than others. The study combined several methods of inquiry, including interviews, focus groups, personal observations, and questionnaires. While multidexterity in research is by no means unusual, there are variations in the degree to which what the left hand of the researcher has done affects what the right hand will do. Some stress studies, for example, have used both interviews and questionnaires, but the latter have been predesigned and were therefore unaffected by interview results.

In theory, different approaches in the same project can fertilize each other, so that data obtained in one fashion can illuminate results obtained through other means. The indepth results of qualitative inquiry, for example, can guide the choices one makes in designing a survey or can illuminate connotations of the responses to one's survey questions. Composite pictures that are drawn from pooled data sources can yield "need assessments," which are definitions of the problem one infers that one ought to be addressing.

The most wasteful approach to data analysis involves compartmentalized cohabitation, in which quantitative and qualitative data are concurrently presented, but never the twain conceptually meet. A contrasting course consists of pooling information so that it becomes difficult to ascertain which inferences derive from which sources. This amalgamation appeals to readers who are allergic to formal research, but not to those who like to see evidence on which conclusions are based. A more fruitful compromise approach is to retain the integrity of data sources but to provide for interconnected-ness of inferences.

In the study reported in this book we began with a qual-itative inquiry and moved to a quantitative one. The quali-tative approach included semistructured in-depth interviews. The main purpose of these interviews was to embed the ex-periences of stress of officers into the overall experience of work life during the course of their career. This goal is sub-servient to our view of occupational stress, which is that the experience can range from being unremitting, as in work that offers unvarying tedium, monotony, and routine—to stress encounters consisting of occasional frustrations and disap-pointments during a fulfilling and exciting career. The differ-ence matters especially where occupations—in this case, po-licing—are frequently characterized in the literature as "stressful."

We deployed focus groups in the study to highlight sources of stress and flesh out their connotations. Focus groups pro-mote "focus," which enhances the contrast between experi-ential figure and ground, and sharpens the contours of com-plaints, in this case, complaints about stress. Focus groups are also "groups," which invites reinforcement of shared ex-periential connotations.

A third qualitative approach we invoked was one of non-participatory observation. We used this approach to garner firsthand impressions about the problems of a subgroup of our informants (female or female ethnic minority officers), who we hypothesized might have distinctive experiences of stress. To conduct these observations we invoked a credible sophisticated observer with an enviable gift for recording and conveying observations.

The results of our qualitative inquiries were used in the way I have suggested—to facilitate the design of a survey instrument and help with the analysis of survey results. The survey was expected to yield numbers, to permit us to de-scribe the magnitude (or relative magnitude) of reported stress experiences, and to compare subgroups of respondents in terms of type and salience of experienced stress.

On another methodological front, we made an effort to involve police as partners in our research. Studies in police departments often feature academics and officers working shoulder to shoulder, but we have gone somewhat beyond this paradigm. We have seen ourselves as helping rank-and-file members of a police organization to understand some of the problems their organization faces and think about ways of solving these problems. This sequence is one that is customarily called organization development (French & Bell, 1999).

Organization development, as defined by its practitioners, prizes the use of data by members of an organization and offers these members the assistance of applied social scientists who are presumed experts in the utilization of data. The collaboration is especially important in organizations that have tended to overvalue "practical experience," with disquieting disregard of the unrepresentativeness of personal impressions. The point of introducing systematic information in such settings is not to downgrade practical wisdom but to supplement it and illuminate it. Ideally, the result that is obtained involves amalgamating native wisdom and scientifically acquired knowledge to the benefit of both.[4]

Our earliest experience with action research in a police department offered an illustration that is a case in point. We were working with a group of police officers in a study of physical confrontations with citizens (Toch & Grant, 1991; Toch, Grant, & Galvin, 1975). After reviewing case records relating to street incidents that had eventuated in the use of

---

[4]The use of data by the members of an organization to define a problem and assist in addressing it is different from the managerial use of data to constrain or control behavior. This difference is highlighted by highly publicized Compstat (crime statistics review) sessions in the New York Police Department, which focus on precinct-by-precinct problems and trends. Flynn (2000) reported that "many commanders say Compstat evolved into an often humiliating experience that seemed more like hazing than brainstorming" (p. B6). Police officers in the same department testified that they experience stress because numerical performance goals that derive from the Compstat strategy alienated them from the citizens they serve. According to Flynn (2000), "officers say that to feel estranged from and deeply mistrusted by the very people they made safe denies them one of the job's greatest satisfactions" (p. B6)

force, the members of our police study group focused on the opening moves of the officers involved. The majority of the group then took the position that the initial approach of almost every officer was foreordained and therefore could not be regarded as a subject for review. The group was open, however, to an effort to document this assumption. The officers took the task very seriously once it was inaugurated, and they constructed an instrument detailing representative situations in which violence could hypothetically result. This questionnaire was then administered (by order of the chief of police) to the entire police department. The data dramatically documented considerable diversity of opinion about appropriate approaches to the situations. Most to the point, the officers discovered sharp differences in views about legitimate approaches between supervisors—including their chief—and many rank-and-file officers. These data proved enlightening for the officers and opened up areas of inquiry that had been previously foreclosed by their "experience"-based assumptions.

The Self-Study Process

We defined our stress project as a self-study project by our participating departments, with ourselves as technical consultants. As I have noted, the job of consultants in a self-study is to provide research expertise (up to and including the writing of books that detail the experience). Consultants in collaborative research projects are additionally presumed to have organizational development skills, so that they can help client groups to define subjects of research and to digest their findings.

Our study involved one police department located in a large city and another in a smaller (suburban) community. For the purpose of planning our surveys, a combined (interdepartmental) task force was set up. This group called itself the Survey Planning Committee. It was composed of nine members and the commissioner of the city department. The key members included men and women, representatives of ethnic groups and three police unions, a captain (subsequently, a second captain), and a sergeant. The suburban police department was represented by the president of its union and one of its female officers.

At the inception of the project, a meeting of the group was held in the commissioner's office. At this meeting, the project was introduced, with emphasis on its self-study procedure. Members of the group enthusiastically endorsed the concept and the subject of the research, which they felt badly needed exploration. They individually expressed strong interest in participating and a determination to work hard to make the project succeed. Several of the officers said they felt flattered to be included as participants.

Our group of consultant–researchers then went our separate ways to gather the qualitative data for our "pump-priming" exercise to provide the officers with a common baseline in designing their survey. I was allocated the task of conducting the formal interviews. My observer colleague, who is a female, African American social scientist, embarked on "ride-alongs" with the female officers, combining informal interviewing and observation. Three other team members set off to run the focus groups, in which they included officers of varying backgrounds.

After the exploratory research work by the consultants had been completed, our formal planning workshop was conducted at a local hotel. On the first day of this workshop, we summarized the impressions we had gained from our explorations. In the second session of this first day, the planning group was asked to nominate the subject matters to be explored in the survey. Each group member was requested to jot down topics on 5" × 8" index cards (as many as desired), to be collated and grouped. The topics that were nominated in this fashion were (a) race- and gender-related stress, (b) departmental administration and "politics," and (c) leadership and communication.

On the second day of the workshop three officer subgroups were to be constituted to draft questions for the survey. These subgroups were to report at the end of the day, and the final selection of the questions was to be made by the total group.

This structured plan for the second day had to be partly

modified when some officers expressed concerns about a possible "hidden agenda" for the study (see chapter 3). The project survived this short-term crisis of trust, emerging with a rededicated congregation and sadder-but-wiser consultants. The officers turned to drafting questions, taking this task immensely seriously and working with intense concentration. By the end of the afternoon, 200 carefully formulated questions had been nominated for inclusion in the survey.

With the questions in hand, we compiled a draft of a questionnaire, which I relayed to the group at its next session. The group reviewed this draft with exquisite and critical care, and suggested a few changes in wording. The questionnaire was revised and then adopted with 46 questions (see Appendix B) and endorsed by the group. The group next considered details of survey administration and decided to route questionnaires through city precinct commanders for distribution. In the suburban department, the survey was to be distributed and collected by the union.

The instrument that was deployed in the suburban department was a shorter version of the city questionnaire. It omitted a few questions (related to racial relations and gender issues) that were inapplicable to the suburban police department.

In the suburb, the union president, who was a member of our planning group, saw to it that the return rate for the questionnaire was 100%. The sample thus corresponds to the population. The return rate in the city department was at first only 25% but was boosted to 30% ($N = 269$) with the help of the union. Table 1.1 compares the city sample to the membership of the department. The table shows that ethnic minority officers are underrepresented in the sample and White officers overrepresented.[5] In other respects the sample appeared to be fairly representative.

---

[5]The problem of a disproportionately low response rate for ethnic minority officers is not exclusive to our study. Haarr and Morash (1999) encountered the same problem and speculated that "the least threatened persons . . . would be most likely to fill out the questionnaire" (p. 317). The corollary of this presumption is that nonrespondents would report more stress than do the respondents if they bothered to respond.

Table 1.1

Comparison of the City Survey Sample and the Uniformed Membership of the Department

Attribute	N	% of sample	N	% of department
Gender				
Female	45	22.1	185	19.8
Male	166	77.9	749	80.2
No response	58			
Race				
Black	39	17.7	219	23.5
White	163	74.1	635	68.3
Hispanic or other	18	8.2	76	8.2
No response	49			
Rank				
Police officer	173	68.1	643	69.8
First line superintendent	38	14.9	103	11.2
Detective	29	11.4	127	13.8
Captain or higher	14	5.5	48	5.2
No response	15			

The city department sample consists of four male officers to every female officer. One third (31%) of the force were officers with bachelor's or graduate degrees, 18% had earned an associate's degree, and 39% had taken some college courses; the remainder (12%) were high school graduates. The suburban sample contained no ethnic minority officers; three members were women and 72% had college degrees. In regard to ethnicity, neither of the two departments is out of line with the constituency it serves. The city population is 64% White, which is roughly the proportion of White people in the department. The suburb, which is a residential adjunct to the city, is 98% White.

After the survey results had been tabulated, arrangements were made for day-long feedback sessions, in which our planning group and other members of the two police departments were supplied with data summaries (heavily consisting of attractively colored pie charts) for their review and analysis. These sessions also doubled as formal ceremonials marking the end of the research project.

Collaborative research is potentially action research, in the sense that outsiders and insiders can try to move from research to action. Actions can then be evaluated through further research (Lewin, 1946). Our work is based on the presumption that if employees are to focus on ameliorating stress or addressing practices that cause or exacerbate stress, this involvement must begin at the stage of diagnosis and specification of the problem. Employees must be invited to participate in formulating the questions to be answered. Once administrators and employees subsequently agree about what the organization is doing that contributes to stress, they can jointly consider what the organization can do to ameliorate these sources of stress.

The degree of participation matters because it affects the extent to which information is "owned" by those who are obtaining it. In discussing this point elsewhere (Toch, 1995), I mentioned 4 desirable attributes for police involved in research:

> First, the question asked should be your question;
> Second, you ought to get the answer yourself;
> Third, there should be closure or task completion; and
> Fourth, the inquiry should carry what you see as meaningful consequences. (pp. 7–8)

With regard to the organization of such research projects, participation calls for team efforts with both sharing and specialization. If consultation is provided to the participants, it mostly ensures that they acquire solid, reliable information from which valid inferences can be drawn.

With regard to the substance of our study, we had been persuaded by Herzberg, Mausner, and Snyderman (1959, 1993) that "satisfiers" and "dissatisfiers" for workers have different sources, with work satisfaction usually deriving from the work itself and dissatisfaction (i.e., stress) from the context of work. Partly to verify this hypothesis with respect to policing, we adopted some of Herzberg's methodology, chiefly in our interviews (see chapter 2). This approach directs attention to the high points and low points of work experience, centering on illustrative vignettes. Where this approach had been used in other studies, incidents that yielded job satisfaction had typically involved valued achievements, and those producing dissatisfaction had centered on issues of administration and on organizational rewards or constraints. The former are variables that are intrinsic to work, and the latter, extrinsic to it.

Stress and Police Reform

In our study, we made an effort to explore the relationship between reported stress and evolving developments in policing. Policing is said to be an occupation that is currently undergoing considerable—some would say revolutionary— change. To the extent to which there is stress among police officers, it is tantalizing to consider whether there are any links between trends in police reform and trends in stress levels. Is any change in police departments stressful? Is the process whereby reforms are enacted a possible source of stress? Do some police officers find change less congenial than others? Do police forces become divided, or even polarized, as a result of reform?

These questions do not apply evenly across police departments. Sometimes police reform is activity that occurs in name only. A cohort of officers may be hired under the rubric of community policing so that federal subsidies can be garnered. The officers may then be trained along traditional lines and assigned standard enforcement activities. Reform in police departments can also become the end of a rainbow. For instance, in many "sweep" (wholesale arrest) and "seed" (community development) operations, the seeding that is supposed to take place never eventuates.

One problem with police reform is the latitude in definitions of terms such as *community policing*, which accommodates a wide range of practices. In theory, community policing presupposes that a police department serves a set of communities and that officers are assigned to neighborhoods where they become familiar with the problems and more responsive to the concerns of residents. For the officers to be responsive to residents, however, the priorities of officers must be partly shaped locally, and officers must enjoy the requisite autonomy. The officers must have leeway to evolve their goals and must work with residents to ensure their responsiveness.

More generous connotations of community policing have to do with an expanded range of police responses to accommodate citizen concerns. Arresting offenders—the time-honored cops-and-robbers game—is often not the best strategy for ameliorating the concerns of the citizens. Creative ingenuity may have to be exercised by the officers for dealing with such problems as truancy, unsafe schools, vandalism, abandoned cars, and vagrants sleeping in doorways. To address these problems, officers may have to work with a variety of agencies that can provide such services as recreational activities, street lights, shelter, and counseling. Officers may have to familiarize themselves with housing codes and foreclosure procedures or learn about substance abuse and homelessness. They may have to invoke new initiatives and coordinate their implementation. They may have to perform functions that require (at least, implicitly) a redefinition of the traditional police role and an expanded conception of policing. Such changes do not come easily in a profession in which rewards (and indices of esteem) have been heavily tied to the pursuit and arrest of malefactors.

Of special interest in connection with police reform is the recent influx of nontraditional (non–White male) officers into police departments and the experiences of these officers. Walker (1992) reported that in the mid-1960s, 3.6% of all sworn officers were African Americans, and as of 1972, only 2% of sworn officers in cities with populations of 50,000 or more were women. By 1986 these figures had risen to 13.5% and 8.8%, respectively. Based on his periodic analysis of police department survey data, Reaves (1996a) estimated that of the full-time sworn officers in local police departments in 1993,

17.5% were members of ethnic minority groups and 10% were women.

Although not many police precincts resemble the melting pots that are often depicted in police television serials (in which ethnic minority officers are invariably in charge of the featured group and White men may be in the minority), diversity in police departments has become the rule rather than the exception. This fact poses questions with respect to stress in policing. We can ask whether newer, nontraditional officers feel unwelcome or resented and therefore define themselves as stressed. Might they feel insecure, inadequate, lonely, rejected, or discriminated against? Might they disapprove of other officers' approach to the job or be disapproved of in turn? Could they have distinct community- or family-related problems?

In our study we have included a department that has undergone diversification and one that has not. Although the departments differ in diversity, both agencies are very much in tune with community-policing philosophies, and they are located in the same geographical vicinity. Both departments were also hospitable to research and concerned with addressing their problems.

Two chapters in this book (chapters 7 and 8) discuss police reform issues related to stress that were not derived from the study of the two police departments. One chapter (chapter 7) deals with what are paradoxical developments in police reform. These trends include the increased involvement of officers in problem-oriented activities, which is mind-expanding for the officers and can increase the satisfaction that they derive from their work. Such involvements can become scintillating manifestations of ingenuity, creativity, and autonomy by officers who have become "experts" in the problem areas they address.

In chapter 7 we deal with the contextual adjustments that may or may not be made in police organizations to facilitate these involvements. We view this question from the perspective of officers who have been temporarily afforded opportunity for enriched work in a progressive but conventional organization. The experience of these officers illustrates the need for continuing congruence between the work and the work context if job satisfaction is to be maximized without risk of stress.

Chapter 8 deals with critical incidents (traumatic experiences such as shootings of officers and by officers) and the amelioration of critical-incident stress through the use of peer-counseling teams. We have included this subject because it uniquely illustrates a model that combines counseling approaches familiar to psychologists and organizational change approaches into a composite intervention. Such an approach seems particularly desirable where some of the context of stress is organizational but consequences involve individual suffering that needs to be reduced.

The intervening chapters are concerned with data obtained from the two police departments in which we conducted our study. Chapter 2 summarizes results of the interviews with officers, which focused on the high and low points of police work. Chapter 3 deals with the officers' definition of stress, as highlighted in focus groups and survey results. Chapter 4 is concerned with issues of stress and gender, which pertain to the municipal police department, and with family stress. It also highlights the relationship between age (the stage of life or career of the person) and stress. Chapter 5 discusses diversity-related problems and conflicts in the city police department, and chapter 6 records the results of data feedback sessions, in which the officers in both departments discussed the findings of our research. Finally, chapter 9 reviews some of our experiences and considers their implications.

2

An Inside View of Police Work

In chapter 1 I mentioned that sources of stress may be over-shadowed by satisfactions and rewards; that problems at work can be frustrating and annoying without being over-whelming, and to enumerate stress-producing circumstances is a far cry from saying that one is unable to cope with them.

At the inception of our research, I conducted focused interviews with the intention of placing the subject of police stress in a broader context. Twenty-two officers were interviewed, including all the officers with whom we worked closely in doing our study. To provide a quantifiable index of the way these officers felt about their departments, I used a self-anchoring scale, in which the ends of the scale (0 and 10) were defined by the officers themselves. A 10—the top of the scale—would be the ideal police department as seen by the respondent. A 0 would be the worst imaginable department.

The ideal police department, as defined by the officers I interviewed, was one redolent with professionalism and efficiency, promotive of fairness and equity, and blessed with responsive and supportive leadership. Least desirable attributes (in rank order) involved political interference, nepotism and inequity, lack of professionalism or blatant incompetence, conflict, and insensitive leadership. Using these criteria, the two departments we studied were rated at the middle-high point of the scale, with respondents divided on the question of whether conditions were improving or deteriorating.

Our interview sample cannot be defended as statistically representative, but we talked with spokespersons for key groups and associations in the departments. Given this diversity, it is interesting that the officers agreed about what makes a police department a desirable or undesirable one. What their responses also suggested was that our research sites were not agencies in crisis or organizations without room for improvement. These inferences are encouraging because a study conducted in a police department with serious morale problems or one in which every officer claims to be deliriously happy would have limited generalizability.

Sources of Work Satisfaction

Research that has focused on high and low points of job-related experiences has documented the fact that sources of job satisfaction in almost all occupations have to do with the work itself (Herzberg, Mausner, & Snyderman, 1993). Our interviews confirm that this intrinsic origin of job satisfaction very much holds for policing. Moreover, the level of enthusiasm expressed in our interviews about the rewards of police work was extraordinarily high. Many testimonials to the excitement of policing studded the responses, including those of officers who in other respects manifested some ambivalence. The following are among the spontaneous remarks made by our respondents:

> You know, we have the greatest job in the world. It is the biggest secret. It really is!
> It's like you live on it. You need it. You look forward to going to work.
> You get out there, and you're playing cops, and you're having a real good time.
> I just feel the joy of this job.

Every emotion that you could ever think of happens to you on this job.
I know that it is not going to be the same day I had yesterday. It is going to be something different. I just enjoy it.
I loved the street. The street was my home. I couldn't get enough of it.

As the officers described what they saw as the high points of their police careers, they recalled a variety of incidents they had effectively resolved, in which citizens received needed assistance. What the officers said they valued was the experience of "walking in and making a difference," "helping somebody who really desperately could use some help," "affecting somebody in some way"—in other words, the opportunity to make a humane contribution.

Providing Assistance to Citizens

In reviewing services they had rendered to civilians in need, some of the officers acknowledged that such incidents were not the stereotypical subject of war stories exchanged in the locker room. The impression the officers conveyed was that the exercise of compassion might be privately valued in policing but that it is publicly unfashionable. This means that an officer's human services work may be a source of pride to him or her but that such accomplishments will not be frequently discussed. One officer put it the following way:

> B5:   I probably wouldn't be telling you this—the good side—if you had not asked me to talk about it. I don't think most police officers talk about it. . . . It's a self thing. It's *you* know it, it's not so much who else knows it. It's *you* know that you did a good thing. Most police officers, like myself, would prefer to talk about the bank robber you caught, the burglar that we caught, or the guy we chased and outran. We tend to elaborate on our stories. The war stories, you know—everybody pumps themselves up a little bit more. Not that it doesn't happen: I've seen police officers do very heroic things. . . .

And yet, when you're a police officer, you see the human side of your fellow officer. You see the cop that hugs the kid, you see the cop that takes the time to talk to the family, to counsel the family if somebody has passed away, you know, who has to walk a tightrope sometimes with emotions just to be able to handle a situation professionally. I see that all the time. They don't give out medals for that. They don't give out awards for that. They don't recognize you for that; they recognize you for catching a bank robber, for chasing down a purse-snatcher.

The contributions that appear most valued by officers occur in calls involving citizens who are manifestly helpless. One such category is that of elderly people, who may be demonstrably fearful, lonely, or confused:

B9:   The old people who have called for years and years and will call and tell you things, and some coppers will say, "Well, what did you call me for, this is stupid. It's stupid, there is nothing we can do." I know the reason they call—it is because they are lonely, they're scared, and they just want a voice, and okay, we check everything, and [say], "How are you doing today?"—we walk out and it is not much, but it gave me a nice feeling. I know somebody else would have blown her off, but I give her her quarter's worth.

* * *

B12:   I liked to be there for every elderly person. I try to treat them like they were my parents or the woman was my mother. You see their side of it, and you bleed for them, and you wish you could make it better. You wish you could make it a Frank Capra picture for them because he always has a happy ending, but unfortunately you can't. We try to do the best we can for them.

* * *

B13:   An elderly man passed away, and naturally his elderly wife didn't exactly know what to do, right? So after the ambulance crew and the fire department left, we . . . sat her down at the table and found out if her husband had any wishes as to a particular funeral director. We called the funeral director, and we started helping her out by calling her relatives. And some of her family who had arrived by then thanked us for helping her out because she didn't know what to do or who to call. That made me feel good that at least I helped this woman out that didn't know up from down in that kind of stressful situation. Any decent person would do something like that, but we get paid for doing that.

* * *

B11:   We find this elderly gentleman, he was lost, and trying to talk to this gentleman, and he just started crying. So we put him in the car and tried to explain to him that we are going to help him. We bring him back to the station, and he is shaking and so forth. I asked him if he had something to eat. He just shook his head. So I went and got him some McDonalds and brought it back for him, and he had a hat on, and I took his hat off and inside the rim of his hat was a name and address. So I pulled out the piece of paper and said, "Is this you?" and he just looked at it. Well, then I put him back in the car, and I went to this address and sure enough that is where he lived and everything, and it just made me feel kind of good. I took care of the man.

Most of the officers proudly recalled occasions involving assistance to children. These included situations of child neglect and circumstances in which services were arranged or brokered by the officers. In some instances, the officers reported they had followed up to make sure that the problem was solved:

B5:   So, you know, I went and talked with the mother for a few minutes and I could tell that this lady was very, very stressed out. She almost had like a blank stare, and she didn't know what to do anymore. . . .

And after spending all that time with her and talking to everybody and interviewing everybody and seeing what's really going on, taking the time to see what's really going on, the most satisfying moment was to see the son come up to the mother and say, "Mommy, I'm sorry," and hugged her, and they were both in tears kissing and hugging each other. I thought, wow, you know, the fact that we were able to be a part of that as a police officer is very satisfying. Anytime that you can help a kid . . . that is rewarding, that in a sense makes up for all the unpleasant things that you have to deal with on this job. . . .

And as a matter of fact we've since followed up and went to see the mother, because I promised them that I would go back. . . . I was able to go back and see the kid, and he was just being a kid again, and the mom was doing great, and I talked to the babysitter and the day-care people and they thought we did a wonderful job. . . . That was one example I walked away from and said it was worth it, you know, I actually got home an hour-and-a-half after I was supposed to get off. . . . You know, to me it was like this is why you do the job.

* * *

B14:   About 4 years ago my partner and I responded to a call where there were accusations being made that a young kid was being kept in his room against his will for approximately 2 years. He was being let out briefly, maybe once or twice a month, to attend school, just to show up. So we went there, and we investigated. . . . It was obvious that he had been kept in there for an extended period of time. We found out that the windows were all boarded up. There were buckets in there [where] he could defecate and urinate, and we investigated that along with the state, and we were able, after research with the state investigation, to find out that this kid—he suffered a mental defect, an aggression defect. Also, his mother, she [had] just come over to this country a couple years before that, and she wasn't used to raising him with the advantages that she would have here in the states, with the counseling and so forth. But we were able to set up help for the family, for this kid, and now today when I see this kid he always recognizes me, and I see the difference, you know, where he could of been, and even the mother appreciates everything [that] took place in that event. . . . We stayed on it for about a good 4 or 5 months, and finally the outcome was that they got a better house and they got turned on to state agencies, counseling, the mother got employed, the kid got put into a school system along with the other kids. You know, where they all benefited from it.

Exercising Interpersonal Skills

Although policing is often equated with the use of legal power or of force, officers appear to take greatest pride in their ability to resolve delicate situations through exercises of verbal ingenuity. In both human services and crime-related incidents, the deployment of interpersonal-relations skills was clearly valued:

> B9:   We were able to talk the guy out, and we took the gun away from him and nobody got hurt. I felt good about that because we could have killed the guy. We chose not to kill the guy. I had several situations like that with people with weapons. . . . If you want to take that as an opportunity, you know, situations where I could have shot people and I didn't, and because I didn't, I reflect that was a good deal. I'm glad we didn't do that. . . . You know, a lot of violent situations you walk into, and through discussions of this and that people put knives down in their houses—whether they would have hurt their spouse or their kids, I don't know. You know, but you leave feeling better than if you hadn't been there —or I know that if someone else had been there, it could have escalated. . . . But those are good feelings when you walk into sometimes tense situations. I left feeling that I contributed and helped. You know, I helped settle that situation.

* * *

> B2:   Now, the mental patient was being very stubborn and didn't want to go in for treatments. They phoned the police. Summoned the police to come over and assist them. . . . No one could understand his language or what

he was talking. He was a former military man, and being one myself, I could identify with what he was saying and what he was going through. So we broke common ground, and I was able to walk him out to the ambulance and being [taken] away without an incident occurring of violence. . . . That was a point in time in my life on the job where I felt I should be at that place and time.

* * *

B12:   Say, some kid that you know in your precinct, or your district, that's constantly been in trouble, and you keep talking to him, "This is what is going to happen to you when you are not a juvenile anymore. You know, you are going to go in jail, and jail is not a fun place to be. You might think that it will make you the big man of the neighborhood, but who is the idiot that is going to be out of the neighborhood?—you are. Your friends will still be here, you know." . . . You know, trying to straighten him out, and when you do see a turnaround in these kids, yeah, that makes you feel good. . . . Give you one example. There was a kid that was always a problem out in North B. Today he is an attorney. . . . Yeah, it is very satisfying for you, you know.

Related high points for the officers involved the exercise of expertise, knowledge, or skills acquired through advanced training and experience:

B7:   Here's the high point. They train me, I'm out here. They send me down to Washington, DC, there are 900 officers, detectives in narcotics, all the way from Scotland Yard—all over the world. And here I'm standing up there telling them about what's it like to be infiltrated into the Jamaican cocaine trafficking. What did I have to do to get accepted by them? . . . All this knowledge that these other people at these high investigative levels respect. They send me to Philadelphia speaking on it.

* * *

B10:   If somebody told me when I was a youngster that you are going to go up and talk in front of 400 people or that you are actually going to teach classes relative to crime, you know, in high school, and then teach classes to little kids about dangerous strangers and sit on the floor and have them crawl all over you and ask you what your night stick is for, I would have thought, oh my God, oh, that will never happen to me and I couldn't do it. Not that I wouldn't have done it. I thought I couldn't do that.

Getting Feedback

Officers appreciate positive feedback from citizens—at minimum, indications that "citizens recognize that you are not the enemy." Officers contend that the experience of civilian gratitude is especially valued because it is hard to come by. As an officer noted, "You have 8-year-olds saying, 'I don't have to tell you nothing, I know my rights,' and when you get someone who actually appreciates you, that is a good feeling."

A second source of feedback to officers is any change or positive result that citizens attribute to their influence or to actions they have taken:

> B4:   I was going into a school where voting booths were being held that day and picking up absentee ballots, and this individual came up to me and, of course, I did not recognize him, and he called me by my name and he just said, "I want to come up and thank you for what you've done, and I haven't had a drink since that night. Me and the wife are getting along." And, you know, it made me feel good that well, here is one of the successes of many times you tried to get people to the right place, that they took advantage of.

* * *

> B19:   An older woman, I think she was 82, her car was stolen, and she was getting her hair done and she is in the middle of the city—doesn't know where she is. . . . She comes out, her car is gone, and she was so upset. She was so sweet, so we put her in the back of the patrol car and said, we will give you a ride home. "Oh, you

would do that for me?" and we said, sure. We took the report, drove her home, and you wouldn't believe it, like two hours later we found her car. That was like the best. She wanted to make us cookies and coffee. "Oh please, you're so sweet," and when we found her car, that was like the greatest thing. It was just the greatest thing to help out someone like that. . . . It is just nice to have, to get a thank you, there is just no respect for us on this job at all.

* * *

B13:   It could be an incident of a little kid walks out of the house, parents don't know, and you grab him on the street because he shouldn't be out there, and you take him home. "Oh, I didn't know he was gone. Oh thank you, thank you," you know, stuff like that. Little things.

* * *

B5:   Maybe just the desire to walk away and say to yourself, whether it's true or not, this person was appreciative. . . . I think that when a person displays appreciation for you coming there and helping them, that's where you get the satisfaction from. You get it from the person's reaction. . . . Also, I think a little bit comes from the fact that you know that what you did was right.

Some officers will go out of their way to arrange for personal contact with citizens, to establish relationships and cultivate good will. This activity can be defined as enforcement-related but is also often regarded as an end in itself:

B10:   With the community policing setup the way that we have it here now, it doesn't really sink into the pores of the city at all. It addresses the squeaky wheel situation. You know, if there is a problem here, take care of it, you know, and then withdraw. . . . Why make it a special unit that talks to kids? I did that for 4 years, and I thought to myself, "We all should be doing this here," you know, and yes, I can get up in front of a group and talk to people, but why can't most of us do it? . . . So what you need to do is to change the department's thinking, the culture of the department. And at the police officer level, you have to really get out there and tell them, "Yeah, our paycheck is coming every two weeks, but you know where the hell it comes from, don't you? It comes from everybody out there, whether you like them or don't."

* * *

B5:   I think a lot of police officers go out of their way to get to know people on the first-name basis and to keep tabs on situations to make sure that they're going okay. It's part of knowing your precinct, it's part of knowing who you're dealing with. You never know when you're going to go back there. You never know when you are going to go back to deal with the situation, and if people are familiar with you—you know, I have found that a lot of times—when you return to a call and when they see you and you were there before, they almost seem a little alleviated because they know that you know, and the first thing they'll tell you is, "You're back." . . . I think we like [for] people when we walk into a place to say, "That's Officer [X]. I know him, he did this for me."

* * *

B12:   Here I am, I'm pushing 46 years old, and if a bicycle detail comes up I'd volunteer for it. You know, when I was a young copper, I enjoyed walking the beat. I loved it. I mean you go in, you talk to the businessmen, people would stop and talk to you. I loved it, and you really don't have that kind of hands-on being in a car because you're just going from call to call.

* * *

B16:   Yesterday, just before I got off work, these little kids were standing on the corner, and a lot of little kids in the rougher neighborhoods are taught not to like the police or don't say hi to the police, or whatever. Well, these two kids did. They said, "Hi, officer," and they were 6 or 7 years old, brother and sister, and I just pulled over immediately. I thought that was very nice and said, "How are you guys doing?" Because usually they look at you and they give you dirty looks and they spit and they do all kinds of gestures, even little kids, but these two kids didn't, and I said, "Do you guys know where there is a store around here?" They said, "Yeah, there is a store right over on the corner." I said, "Are you guys old enough to go there? Are you allowed to go there?" They said, "Yeah, yeah." You're going to think I am nuts, but I took a dollar out and I said, "I found this dollar and you know, I can't think of nobody else better to buy a candy bar than you two guys," and I gave them the dollar, and I said, "Go buy yourself a candy bar." I don't know why. . . . I just liked the fact that they said hi to me. That just made my day.

During our study, one officer died and his partner was seriously injured in a shooting. The aftermath of this incident was a period of improved relationships between officers and citizens, which some officers thought was an ironic (although welcome) twist of fate.

B19: The days leading up to his funeral, the hand-shakes, and the pats on the back, and the cups of coffee, and people were bringing us food left and right, and the thank-yous, "We just never thanked you" and, you know, "I lived in [Precinct] B 20 years and never had to call the police and to realize what you people go through." It was unbelievable, and for three days it was just, oh my God, this job isn't half bad—people are actually appre-ciating us. It was a sad time, but in another sense, it was nice being thanked and, unfortunately, something like that had to happen to feel a little appreciated.

Receiving Peer-Group Support

The officers cited two sources of satisfaction that had to do with peer support. One focused on the solidarity and loyalty of the police force; the other, on relationships with partners and other work associates. The following are examples of comments that highlight rewards having to do with belongingness, solidarity, and support:

> B7:   But see, there is that fraternal organization that I belong to. If I put out a call for help, the officers will be there. I tell people all the time the greatest thing I have is that I know that I could put a call out for 911 off duty or on duty, and I am going to get a great response. . . . Most times, if an officer-in-trouble call comes out, I don't care what you are doing, it drops. If you're eating, you stop. You're pulling up your pants coming up the stairs. They will be there. I love it when I am out on call, and if I see the door's open, I have to get back on the radio. Radio in that me and my partner are getting ready to go into the building—we found the front door open. I know that within 30 seconds I am going to hear another car pull up. They are going to back me, and that is very grand. That's very supportive and that makes me feel good and that has nothing to do with [me] being a black man or anything. It is, I [am] going into that house as a fellow police officer, that is good. If I put out a call that I am in a fight, I got an officer-in-trouble call, me and my partner need backing, I know that within 30 seconds I am going to hear cars coming, and when they get there they are not going to say, well this is black-on-black, it is white-on-black [violence]. They are going to get out there and they are going to dissolve the problem that is surrounding me quick. And I feel good about that.

* * *

> B20:   What really gives me a sense of satisfaction, too, is the people that I work with. The camaraderie that they have; it is a really tight-knit group, and I like that. At work and out of work it is a very tight-knit group. . . . Probably some of the closest friends I have ever had in my life, even in such a short period of time. . . . You have a common bond. You all deal with the same situations, occasionally dangerous situations, and you kind of have an understanding of what the other one goes through.

* * *

B14: I found the loyalty, the friendship, which I probably didn't know existed when I was young, was a part
of this job; soon after I got on I found it. I found no
matter what kind of background I had or what color I
was, there was a sense of loyalty because we were all in
the same profession.

* * *

B10: The guy thing about being able to go and trust
your partner, and nothing else matters, so you trust them
because that's what we're talking about out there.
I: So you know that there is always backing?
B10: Yeah, that is part of the good feeling that we cops
feed off. Very, very strange people. You may or may not
have caught the drift of that, but when you interview
cops, we are basically pretty strange.
I: So that's a continuing source of satisfaction.
B10: Just being part of it.

Sources of Work Stress

Past research on the subject leads one to expect that most
sources of stress for the officers would consist of pressures
and demands that originate in the context of their work and
in their personal lives as these impinge on their job. These
expectations are confirmed (at least, in part) by responses we
obtained in other parts of our study that are reviewed in the
chapters that follow. In our interviews, however, the low
points most frequently mentioned involved the work itself—
experiences relating to injury, death, and suffering.

Death of a Child

The most anguished accounts of painful experiences by the
officers involved incidents in which children had lost their
lives. In such accounts, some of the officers mentioned ago-
nized ruminations during and following the events; others
referred to the lasting impact of their experience. One officer
described two adolescent shootings he had witnessed:

B5:   I remember going to a call of a shooting, and there on the sidewalk was this kid gurgling, breathing his last breath. I'll never forget the look on that kid's face because it's the first time that I'd ever seen a person dying. . . . I went home thinking just how this kid died. Just how sudden his life was over, and how there was nothing that I could do or anybody could do to save him, and that is always hard to deal with. Because it seemed to me that's so senseless. I have children, I have a teenager, and to wake up one day and to even live with the thought that she's not around any more, to me it's like that would be the most devastating feeling in my entire life, and so at the same time, I remember standing there thinking, I can't let this bother me. I can't let this bother me because I'm a police officer. Police officers don't show emotion, and police officers don't show the public that this bothers them. I remember putting up that facade and talking to the guys next to me almost with a lump in my throat thinking, this kid just died in front of me. He died because somebody felt like shooting him in the head three times.

*   *   *

B5:   It was an accident, and when we got there, there was a young 15-year-old kid laying on the floor, and you looked at his face and you could tell he was gone. There was no color in his face, and I remember the ambulance people coming in. There was a bunch of other kids in there, and I was trying to get information from them, and I remember the ambulance people coming in and heard them start opening his shirt up and start working on him. I remember as they were trying to resuscitate him, he had this gaping hole in his stomach, and you could see the intestines and everything through the hole every time they gave him the compression. And, you know, it wasn't so much the gore that bothered me, just again the fact that, Why is this happening? Why [did] a 15-year-old die like this? Why did these kids even have a shotgun? And then the frustration of trying to get information and not having people who were there give you the information.

* * *

B5:   It is a feeling, it's a sad feeling, it's a feeling of why, you know, why? It's senseless. I guess a lot of people say that. You know, whenever somebody dies, there [are] never enough words, and there [are] never the right words. And that's one thing to deal with, but also dealing with the fact that you were there. That maybe you were the last face this kid saw. You know, maybe you were the last voice he heard asking him questions. I remember leaning over the first kid I told you about, I remember leaning down and trying to talk to him and trying to get a response out of him, and I almost got the feeling that he was looking at me but couldn't say, couldn't speak—he was trying to, and I'm thinking jeez, you know, I was the last person this kid saw, and I couldn't help him. He's probably no older than my own kid, and I couldn't say to him, you know, his parents never said to him "Goodbye," never.

I don't know what the relationship was with his parents—and again, when you're a family man and your family is the most important thing to you, and you know, you see this senseless waste of a human life like that, it kind of hits home. It hits home because it becomes a part of you. I heard somebody said, some officer said on TV one time, you know, this job takes little pieces of you. It does. You remember a few incidents, and they just like become a part of you and sometimes they take a piece and sometimes they put a piece back. . . . I think they all stay with you, and I think that some days they all come back, and on most days you don't think about them because you are preoccupied with other things, but on the day it gets bad, they all come back.

The traumatic impact of police experiences—especially when these involve children—can be compounded by the nature of the police task, which requires a show of imperturbability. The need to keep emotions in check can produce psychological strain, as can the feeling of impotent anger that officers may experience when they find themselves forced to play the role of spectators to human tragedy:

B5: We had a hanging, he hanged himself, and you know, the only thing that I could think of to deal with it —because I thought this is so horrible that a person should get to this point in their life where they feel that they have to end their life this way, you know—the only thing that I could think of, was to just pray at the moment and just say, "Lord, do you know why this happened?"

* * *

B19: It was a call of attempted suicide, and we happened to be a minute or two away, and we pull up and the mother is screaming at the door, "My son is in the bedroom. I think he shot himself." And we go in, and it happens that he was sitting on a waterbed, and there [are] the bookshelves on the headboard, and there [are] brain matter and blood, and you have the mother who is hysterical, the daughter who is trying to come in the room, and we are trying to push them out. . . . It was the strangest thing. I will never forget it. As I was standing there and parents and family members were going in the other room and officers were assisting them, looking right at me in the hallway was this child's school pictures. I walked over, and I actually took them down and set them down and turned them over; it was the weirdest thing. I don't know why I did it, if it was for the family, for officers, for me—I don't know why.

* * *

B15: I watched life leave a young lady's eyes at 5 o'clock in the morning, that one day. She was a street walker, and someone had chopped her across the head with a machete, and we called for an ambulance, and she was on someone's porch, and she was nude from the waist down, and she was banging on the door, and they called the police. I mean, she just said, "Help me, please just help me," and I was holding her head and looking into her eyes and telling her, "You will be all right, we'll call for an ambulance," and I am screaming in the radio for the ambulance to come. And it was too late, and I feel that I am six feet, and I am big, and I am Black, and I am bad, and there is nothing that I can do, and so that sense of powerlessness, against forces that are greater than you, sometimes you say, "This is enough, and I don't want to see this sort of thing," and I mean, I can remember her face very clearly and very distinctly, and it really wasn't until I started working in the EAP [Employee Assistance Program] that I was able to talk about this without getting all teary-eyed because it would . . . it bothered me in that sense.

* * *

B11:   You know, I am human. If you are not human, then there is something wrong. Naturally it is going to bother you. Certain things that you do . . . Like in one instance, a call came out on the east side where a gentleman had his little boy hostage, so we called in on the call and by the time we got there, he had already killed his son, and what he did, he stuck a machete right through his body and had it embedded into the ground. We got there, and you look at that. It just makes you sick. Okay, I mean this is what I am saying, you see things like that, especially if it is a child, that is what really bothers me, and again you got to be in it to understand what it is, and you never forget anything like that.

* * *

B23:   Had a car chase, and they chased them up G Street and made a left turn on L and a police car behind them. Sunday services, and a 10-year-old kid came out between two parked cars and nobody saw him and boom, he was killed. That is the day that I said I would never chase another car.

* * *

B16:   Well, I happened to be right in front of it, so I pulled into the parking lot on a motorcycle, and what had happened is this lady was pulling up to the front of the store and apparently her brakes had failed and another woman was walking with her child in a stroller from another store, and the car had crushed the child between the car and the wall and, well, I just got the car off the baby, and the stroller was like twisted, crushed.

It was a metal stroller with the canvas, and I pulled it apart and tried to do whatever I could do for the baby. It was lifeless, basically, at the time, and then shortly thereafter the ambulances came and all that, and they took the child to the hospital, where the baby died. But instances like that tend to stay in your mind a long, long time.

* * *

B11:   So we went to the house, and it was traffic warrants out of Pennsylvania [to arrest a man for unpaid traffic tickets]—nothing major. Explained everything to him. His wife was there with their three children, and one was, I guess, about a year-and-a-half, the other one about 3 months old, and the other one was about 13. So the little baby I picked up and held in my arms for a little while. We were explaining everything. So we brought him downtown.

I: The father?

B11:   Right. So it was about 4 days later. I come home from work. The newspaper is on the table. I see the picture. See the picture in the paper of this other officer, that we assisted with the warrant, leading the mother out of the house. She had killed her two little kids. That is all I could picture, is holding that little baby, and that really got to me, you know.

Other Traumatic Experiences

Police work places its practitioners into disproportionate contact with human nature at its worst and requires them to become inured to the predation and violence they encounter. Having to deal daily with violent acts, however, does not mean that one becomes indifferent to the suffering of victims. Child abuse or child neglect rank especially high among experiences that are described by officers as traumatic:

B19:   It was a sad day as it was, and then we had a child neglect. A 2- and 3-year-old were outside naked, and it was a cold day, and there was a 7-month-old baby sitting on the couch, and they were probably like that for a couple of hours, and you realize this is how the world is, and you can't save the world, so for that time you are only in their lives for a few moments—20 minutes, an hour—and you try to do the best you can. You hope somehow it makes a difference, and I could choke and it frustrates me when I know I go home that night and my son is fed, is bathed, is ready for bed, and these poor children, you don't know what is going to happen to them.

We thought the baby was only about 2 months old because the baby was only about this big, and the baby was just sitting, stiff as a board, wide awake, just didn't know. Obviously was never held, never cuddled, just sitting there sweating, and the other ones had no clothes on, and there wasn't a toy in the house; there was one bottle of mustard in the refrigerator—that was it. There was two garbage bags broken open in the middle of the floor with chicken bones, and it looked like an abandoned home.

* * *

B6:   Well, the one that comes to mind is really a child that would talk to nobody else within the whole system, and the only one that that child felt safe with was with me, and I just remember that face. And the other child I remember is simply because of what was done to him. It was a boy, and they cooked him in the oven a little bit here, and going through the system with that, that had an impact because of just what was done to the child. . . . They wrapped cords around his neck and stuff, so that stuck to my memory. I didn't sleep for a while after that.

Empathy with victims can plausibly lead to burnout, as victimization experiences cumulate. One must also deal with the continuing realization that many perpetrators of violence will never be apprehended and cannot be brought to justice:

B12:   Talk about frustration, that is really frustration where you beat your head against the wall trying to get somebody that you know did something to somebody. I mean, I worked almost three years in the Sex Offense Squad investigating rapes and child molestation, and I mean, you know, that was the tough part. [And] there was nobody to blame. Other than you felt bad for the people that came to you for help and you couldn't help them—you take it personally after a while. Then there are times where it starts getting to you and you go, "Well now, it's time for a change," so you go somewhere else.

* * *

B12:   You try to rationalize in your head, how can somebody do something like that to somebody this young? ... It aggravates you, and you go home really feeling frustrated and mad about the whole situation, and after a while you learn that there are things that you can't control.

At the beginning, it was new, and you can shut off when I was working in that particular squad. But then, after a while, you really couldn't. It starts bothering you, and you know, the people that I worked with back there, they are still there and you know, I give them all the credit in the world for staying there as long as they did. ... I think it is possible to become hard, you know, and like I said, it was tough for me because at the time I had three small boys. I mean, if I wasn't a police officer what would I do as a parent if somebody did that to my child, you know? And I happen to think as a police officer if I really wanted to do that, you know, I could probably get 10 years.

Problems With Partners

Police officers can sometimes pinpoint sharply delineated periods of high stress. One source of such high-stress experiences involves being assigned to work with a difficult or uncongenial partner. (As aficionados of police procedurals know, patrol officers who work together become closely interdependent. The corollary of this fact is that nonintersecting habits or attitudes can become extremely problematic for partners.)

Police officers who are habitually overaggressive or prone

to conflict spell trouble for those who work with them. Violence-prone officers are therefore assiduously avoided by their peers. The following plaintive excerpts delineate the problem that such a partner represents when he cannot be avoided.

> B9:   There were days that I was apprehensive to come to work. I mean, I would take days off—I would have to take a day off.... I would work with the same individual for 8 days, and sometimes I would have to take a day off in the middle of those 8 days just to get away from him because I needed to get away from him. I mean, you would get in the car, and the guy had such a bad temper that the littlest thing could set him off, and you just didn't know what was going to set this individual off.
> I: So he was out of control?
> B9:   He was crazy, he was crazy.... I felt he was very capable of hurting people, and it made me very nervous. I would keep him away from certain situations. We just wouldn't cover certain calls because I knew he would get in the middle of it.
> I: Was he aware of the fact that you were doing this?
> B9:   Yeah, he didn't care.

> * * *

> B9:   It was very uncomfortable and somewhat stressful. You know, I would say, "Gee, you should really watch your temper on that last one" and laugh a little bit, and he would say, "Yeah, but I didn't kill him." I mean, no matter what I said and no matter what he said, his personality never changed. He was always a potentially explosive individual.... Keep him away from people was the only thing that would keep him calm. And after a while I just accepted that sort of my role here for now was ... I was his babysitter, and I would tell the other car crews that, and they would say, "Thanks, don't dare bring him around."

> * * *

> B9:   He told me that "They don't want me to do my job.

So I won't do my job," and I said, "Well that's good, fine, don't do your job. We will ride around in a circle and we'll talk to girls or stare at the trees, you know," and I would just hope that he wouldn't get into a situation where somebody really pissed him off.

* * *

B9:   You couldn't stop cars because he would get in an argument in a heartbeat with someone and you just didn't know—the guy had such an explosive temper. You wouldn't dare do something at the risk that this guy would go off the handle and not only hurt somebody, but put you in a very bad situation that I would have to then try to justify. How in God's name did you do that? And so I was the one that would kind of drive around and keep him from things. . . . But any given day, had I gone in and said, "Today let's go, you know, stop 10 cars and arrest 12 people," he would have been happy to do it. God knows what would have happened if we did it.

In most instances, complaints about partners have to do with individuals whose personal problems affect their work. In such instances the cycle is one in which one person's stress manifests itself in a way that creates stress for a second person:

B18:   It was a little tough. Because every day I would go home with a headache, just from her ranting an l raving, and it was like, I shouldn't have to go home with a headache because she was going crazy today and like a maniac pulling people over because they cut her off and stuff like that. That is not the way.

* * *

B15:   They partnered me with another older officer, who was very bitter behind a divorce, and he would get no pay for two weeks because his wife was getting all of his money. So with him being bitter and me being bitter, it just fed on each other. At that point . . . I felt that this job sucks, I am out of here the first chance I get.

* * *

B13:   They, more than likely, already know before I get involved with this person what this person is like. It is just that somebody has to be with this person, and it is just that I am the unlucky one that particular time to be with him. Now, there are some people that you get in the car [who] won't talk the whole day that you are with them. There are other people who talk your ear off. Some people don't want to ride with people who will talk your ear off. Me, it doesn't bother. I'll close my ears so I don't hear them. . . . But there are certain things in your structured life, where you figure it is wrong, isn't supposed to happen, and you're not supposed to do. I mean, how far can you push your tolerance?

Problems With Supervisors

Like partners, first-line supervisors can be stressors or sources of stress that directly impinge on the officer. Among other resaons, an irritating supervisor has to be faced daily; he or she cannot be avoided. As one officer put it,

B3:   I don't think it's true just in police work. I think it's true if you're digging a ditch. I think that the person that has the most effect on your life is the person who is immediately ahead of you, the first person you have to report to; your first supervisor has the biggest impact in your life. Sometimes more so than your family. . . . I think that how he makes your day at work is gonna affect you the most. Because I might not see the guy at the top for a month, but I see this guy every day, and if every day I come to work he is making my life miserable or I'm not getting what I think I need or he's not helping . . . and when the worker isn't getting that, I think that is when he goes home and that's when he drinks and that is when he has his problems. I think it's true in any area of employment. . . . I think the majority of stress any worker has got to deal with is his first line of supervision. I think that person plays the most important role.

As with partners, relationships with supervisors can degenerate, and the parties involved can become sources of stress for each other. Differences in power, however, give supervisors an edge when it comes to being stressful. A supervisor can harass a subordinate, leaving him or her feeling impotent and without resources:

> B16: I probably was only about a year or two on the job, and I had a lieutenant that, to me, I had absolutely no respect for the guy. And with my military background, I like to have respect for a person because I feel that they know more than me . . . but this particular individual had no leadership qualities, he was totally unethical. . . . And he put me on a walking beat 5 or 6 years on the job.
>
> I: So he took it out on you?
>
> B16: Yeah, so he put me on the beat every night and checked on me every 10 or 15 minutes to make sure I was out there, in a bad part of town, all by myself; for about 6 months that lasted.
>
> I: And you were completely helpless . . .
>
> B16: Basically, yeah. He was the lieutenant, and I was new, fairly new on the job, and I had to do what I had to do. . . . It was just his way of saying, "I am still the lieutenant, and you're not going to tell me I'm a coward because you're a police officer." . . . I dreaded going to work everyday. I would look outside and see the snow coming down and I would say, oh my God, I am going to be out there for 8 hours. And I was afraid, at the time, that I would say something to him and get in trouble, because a couple of times I came in and I was cold, so I would have to make an excuse just to use the bathroom or something, just to get warmed up, and a couple of times, I didn't say it in a nice way, either. I'd say, "I am here to use the bathroom," and he would go, "Okay, as soon as you're done, then go back out," and he would look at his watch, and you know, that is the way it was.
>
> I: So this thing was getting kind of hairy?
>
> B16: Yeah, oh yeah, it was stressful at the time, I was at my wits' end there.

Concerns relating to higher level administrators are opposite to those focused on immediate supervisors. Whereas the latter are viewed as intrusive, the former can be perceived as disengaged. Police executives who have risen through the ranks (as most have) are accused of having forgotten what the job is like and portrayed as insensitive—or indifferent, or both—to the needs of officers.

> B9:   They are not policemen. The people in this building are not policemen, all right? They don't, most of them wouldn't even know how to be a policeman, and I don't say that bitterly. It is just how it is. Some are good book guys, you know, studied and very quickly moved up the ladder, but because they chose, they didn't like doing that and they wanted to do this. I don't have a problem with that. I don't have a problem with what they are doing. They run the department and they get the grants and they do all the pencil pushing. That is fine, but they are not policemen.

* * *

> B16:   It is hard to go by rules that were made by some-body who was never sitting where I am sitting, for me. I mean I go by them only because I have to, to get a paycheck, but I don't like it necessarily.

* * *

> B19:   People higher up in the department who haven't been on the street for years and years, who come down with some rules and regulations—where you go, what are you thinking? Come out and ask us before you make a decision! Come out to the district and say, "Well, we're getting police cars, what would you like in the car to make it more comfortable?" You sit in a car for 10 hours. When you put the radios in, it would be nice if you leave some room to pull the cup holders up. One little thing —and there are no cup holders, now you got hot coffee in your hand and you can't put it anywhere. The cars, you have, like, the velvet seats up front and they put them in the back. Now you get prisoners that unfortu-nately wet themselves and you can't wash the back seat

of the car out. Just put vinyl seats in the back seat—just something like that.

I: And you think you would be able to predict this?

B19:   Oh sure, because we deal with it all the time.

The Reward System

The strongest feelings of frustration that are expressed by officers focus on perceived inequities in the system whereby promotions and other rewards are allocated. The description of the problem revolves around "politics," which denotes a variety of ways in which the process is assumed to be tainted (see chapter 3). Some officers claimed that their concern about the fairness and equity of the process had made them bitter and disaffected and diminished their commitment and work motivation.

> B3:   The good people aren't putting in for the jobs any more, aren't putting in for the promotions any more; unfortunately, what I might consider to be some of the bad people are going to be the only alternatives. You know, people with no people skills at all who are just there to further their own ends are going to be in the position where they can do that. . . . I've watched their careers as long as I've been here, and they've always been self-serving, and now they're going to be in positions to be really self-serving, and they just have no compassion for the men who work beneath them, and they're going to be in charge some day.

* * *

> B10:   If they could shaft you, then they are shafting the citizens, because first of all if they don't believe in you, then they don't believe in the citizens to start with. And the second part about that, and the real down part of that, is if you're feeling good about yourself, you will do a good job. If you are not feeling good about yourself, you wind up down there. So you're talking about working conditions.

* * *

B14:   It's to the point where I try to get to work every day at least an hour before I start, to get myself physically and mentally prepared to work. I am at the point now that I don't even like coming to work. I have changed shifts . . . because I saw myself getting an attitude, where I didn't like going to work, I didn't like giving 110% of myself at 4 o'clock to 2:00 in the morning, where it is much more dangerous, so I decided to come on the slower shift because I am not going to give as much, because I am not going to get rewarded for it. I am going to go there and get a paycheck. This is primarily why I work, but I miss the action of the evening. I still have the dedication, and I still have knowledge for that job, but I am at the point now where (and it is bad, because this is a slower shift, slower time of day), I don't even like coming to work. I don't even like coming to work.

And it is not because of what I do out on the street. I can deal with just about anything out there on the street. I am not the biggest, I am not the baddest, I am not the strongest man in the world, but I am getting mentally reserved about this job because of the politics, and that is all it boils down to. . . .

I saw myself out there with my life and possibly my partner's life on the line, and no matter what we did, no matter how good we did it, or how bad we did it, we were not going to be rewarded for it. And I didn't want to jeopardize my life, my family's life, and another human being's life and not be patted on the back. When I see the same person that didn't care, didn't have the knowledge and dedication that I had, but had the influence and the bucks. So why make myself look like a fool? . . . Last Sunday, I sat down and talked to more experienced coppers that have been on this job, and I got their opinion, because I am considering quitting after 9 years.

I: It bothers you that much?

B14:   It bothers me that much, and I have talked it over with my wife and my family, and my wife is behind me 110%, and if it continues to bother me and starts to stress me out—and it is starting to stress me out—to where I don't like coming to work, and that is unheard of for me because I have never considered myself a quitter—but I am considering myself a quitter because it is just affecting me mentally and physically. . . .

I: Why do you think that some of this tension is developing?

B14: Politics. . . . From my point, it is the White guys are getting promoted that are politically connected, and a White man that is sitting in this chair probably will say that it is the minorities that are getting promoted because we have to fill a quota now, with this affirmative action. . . . Well, my impression is that I see incompetent White guys, incompetent Black guys, incompetent White females, incompetent Hispanic females, Black females getting promoted all over, and I am not trying to make it one-sided. I don't want to make it a racial issue.

I: The issue is incompetence and political connections irrespective of race, creed, or color?

B14: Yes sir.

Time Pressures and Constraints

Being stressed can mean that one is understimulated or overstimulated. On the average, police stress in a large city is of the latter variety. Although officers in theory spend time patrolling their beats, they may instead find themselves careening uninterruptedly from one incident to the next. Beyond the frenetic pace this routine may entail, the officer may feel constrained in his work, knowing that as he deals with one incident, his services may be in demand at the next.

B12: My particular sector, there is only one car working. Some of the sectors have two, two cars working. If I am responding to my call, I am at my call and I am trying to advise people. Right away, if your 20 minutes or whatever is up on a call, they are right there. "Car"—let's say —"Delta 100, are you back?" Now you got to radio, "We are still out." Okay, so now you got to try and get to this next call. You know, well, if you had more car crews working, you wouldn't have these stackable calls. . . .-

And if you think you can guide that person in 5 or 10 minutes, there is no way in hell you can do it.

* * *

B12:   On occasion you are going to have to leave this call, and you're going to have to go to *this* call, this is a higher priority call. So you have to leave these people and go there. Civilians don't understand priority. They think their problem is priority, okay. . . . So you know, in some situations it puts you between a rock and a hard place. That is, I think it is, you know, very frustrating. . . .

I said civilians don't want to hear that. You're there, and they want your help. They want your advisement, and the dispatcher is only doing his job. The computer casts this and says, "Well, this is a Priority 4." This one here is going to be a Priority 1. So you are going to have to leave this and go to the other one. . . .

You know, people who have neighbor problems, they have problems with their neighbors. So, you know, you're not going to just talk to the one neighbor, they are going to give you their side, the complainant. You are going to want to go over and talk to the neighbor and try to get their side. Try to mediate this thing the best way you can. . . . But I think that if you had more police working, you wouldn't run into that problem.

* * *

B12:   Where we are, there are a lot of senior citizens. You know, in my district. So you know it's kind of tough, because, number 1, they don't understand. Times changed, society changed and, you know, they don't really understand that, and they figure they are there and they want your help, and they want you to sit there and try to explain it to them where they can comprehend it as much as they can. But like I said, when you get that, "Are you back yet?" you know, you really don't want to end abruptly. So you really try to make sure that they understand, and sometimes if I don't think they do I try to get back to them if I can.

If I have a free moment or if I don't have another call to go on, you know, I try to get back to them. You know, people my age or the kids younger, you know, you can deal with them kind of fast, but the older people you got to take your time with it, and some of the dispatchers now are civilians, so, you know, they weren't out there. They weren't trained out there. They don't know. They figure, I guess they figure, "Well, I got a call here CAD [computer-assisted dispatch] says it is a Priority 2, you are going to have to leave this one, and you are going to have to go." So it gets to be a bit of a dilemma at times, and sometimes I feel badly about it, which I do when it comes to the elderly. Christ, I have a mother who is in her 70s. I wouldn't want a copper to go to her and say, "Well look, just do it this way, and I got to go—I got another call to go on now, you know?" I'd be taken aback a bit. You know, I try to be as sympathetic as possible and make sure that both parties understand.

I: As a senior citizen I want you to know that I appreciate this.

* * *

B12:   There are times that they don't want you to leave. I mean, you explain to them that there is another call that I got to go on, and, "Well, I don't understand this." . . . I say, "I have to work between guidelines, you know, the criminal element, they have no guidelines to follow. I have to follow them." So you try to make them understand and hopefully give them some kind of peace of mind, when we can—and the other thing is when you're going, you're getting calls, and you're going from pillar to post. I mean, it is very hard to try and patrol and just do a patrol to make sure that everything is all right in your sector. But that is kind of hard when you only got a car working in that sector, or if you get too tied up where you feel you are going to make an arrest, well, then you got to tell radio, "I think I am going to be going down with an arrest," and then hopefully there is another car available who they can give that call to. . . . The city is strapped, and it's like everything else, you're told to do the best you can with what we have.

I: Which is discouraging?

B12: Very discouraging.

A related issue is that of the variety of calls, which may feature disparate stimulation levels and seesawing physiological demands. A case can be made—as in the following —that this type of roller-coaster routine is a ready-made recipe for stress:

> B7: Now, think about it, you're sitting in a police car, you drive around, you wait on your calls, and you go up and down the street, and you're looking for crime, you're being visible, but you get a call to go take a report, you go take a report. You get a call that somebody fell out of their bed and needs help to get put back in their bed.
>
> This thing about being a police officer is that hidden call, that you just don't know when it's coming. That call that says there is a shooting over here, and now you got to go there, and when you get there you know that this is real, and when you walk in there, and you see that there are two or three bodies that have been shot up, and you do your part as the profession, you secure the scene, you investigate, and you do all that and at the end you call yourself [you radio in your status], "Bravo 240, back in service." Nobody tells you to go home when you've been part of a scene like that. Nobody tells you, "Well, I am going to give you the day off, now you go home and regroup yourself because you've seen something very ugly today." Somebody tells you at the end of the call, "Call yourself back in service; you be ready for the next one."
>
> So your body emotionally is going up and down. This is 7:00 a.m. and you get a call DOA, dead on arrival, somebody who dies in the neighbor's house, and who has just died. But here again, how many people wake up in the morning in their profession, and you go to somebody's house and you walk in there, their family is destroyed, here you got a body? You make sure there is nothing criminal that is there. It is just okay. Now you make your phone calls. You spent an hour-and-a-half in the room with a body in the bag. I usually, you know,

say my prayers for the family, and I make my condolences. Now you go back, nobody tells you, "Okay, we realize it is 7:00 a.m., we didn't expect you to have that DOA and all, so why don't you take 2 hours off and kind of get yourself back together?" When you say, "Bravo 240 is back in service," you go to your next call. Now the next call can be, guess what? "Bravo 240, you got another DOA." Nobody is going to say, "Wait a minute, you got your one for the day. So we are going to give this to another car crew." It don't work that way. You still gotta go there and you still gotta eat lunch; I don't know about everybody else, but what happens if you just spent the last 90 minutes looking at a suicide? You're still hungry. You still got to eat.

So now you go home at the end of the day, and this is where that drinking and all starts to come into play. Because you have all these other calls and you never know when that call comes, and you're flying down the streets at 60 mph, and you got to try and stay calm, and you got to try to get to where you're going without tearing up that car or injure yourself or somebody else, and then when you get there you find out that it was a fake call. Okay, calm down, get your emotions back down here, okay, because you just flew the last mile and a half at 60 mph thinking that you were going on a fight or a violent domestic, and when you get there you find out that it was nothing, but you now got to come on back down. Now get ready for your next call. Next call, some little old lady has locked herself out of her car. So that emotional level for a police officer is up, down, up, down, and that's that stress that starts. You don't know it. All of a sudden you find after work that you start drinking more. You find yourself a little edgy.

Issues of Self-Efficacy

Police work is very complex professional work that requires officers to exercise considerable skill, make delicate decisions with fateful consequences, and solve a wide range of interpersonal problems, with no hard-and-fast criteria about the

correctness or incorrectness of solutions. Officers must therefore live with doubts and uncertainty about some of what
they have done, which can make them question their own
adequacy or competence and undermine their self-esteem:

> B23: You know what stress is on this job? People not
> knowing that they did it right or they don't know. They
> just don't know, and they went by the seat of their pants
> to do it on a call, and that is what it is. They don't know
> if they made the right choice or the bad choice. . . .
>
> Maybe you stopped a car and you let them go and you
> say, "Oh Jesus, I bet he had a gun or something." It is
> just, you got to feel comfortable on this job. You have to
> feel this job. There is nobody there to show them. I mean,
> you can take any situation and you probably could make
> it into six different scenarios, like six different answers.
> Well, that ain't the way it is out there. I mean, you get a
> situation, you have to solve this problem, sometimes you
> can't, but you have to do something to solve this dispute.
> You can't just turn around and say, "Well, this is too
> much for me. I can't take this," and walk out. And you
> have to know how to handle people.

* * *

> B20: And I don't think I made the right choice. I think
> I should of went in and that bothers me. . . .
> I: In fact, it wouldn't have made any difference?
> B20: Well, maybe not; maybe it would have. That is the
> question. That is the question that I have to deal with.
> I: You're still bothered by this?
> B20: Yes.
> I: You will always be bothered by this?
> B20: Probably.

* * *

> B12: I believe that my performances were always ade-
> quate. It's just that there's circumstances where you run
> into a brick wall. You will have hot leads, and then your
> leads will get cold. You have drive-by shootings going
> on, you might have somebody out there that knows ex-
> actly what happened but won't tell you. You may get

frustrated, but that is not because of my inadequacies. I am out there doing my job and doing it the best way I know how. I don't think that I personally fail these people. I take it upon myself, for I feel that I let them down because I ran into a stone wall some place. It is not that I wasn't out there doing my job. I did my job the best way I can. The best way I know how. It is just that, unfortunately, you run into legal things that prevent you from it. . . . You explore every avenue. And I mean, out of all my cases, I've explored and exhausted every avenue. So as far as myself, I don't believe that I have any inadequacies, as far as that goes, other than I take these things personally and sometimes I shouldn't, but that is just me. . . . It's just that sometimes things bother me and they shouldn't. Maybe I am a little bit too sensitive on things, I can't help that—that is just me—but I don't think that makes me a bad police officer.

A related problem can arise when other people (such as disgruntled offenders) raise questions about the officer's efficacy, and these questions are taken seriously by the organization, leaving the implication that the officer's supervisors give credence to the charges.

B5:   I remember going home thinking, "Is this going to happen every time somebody that I lock up that doesn't like me or that, you know, feels I did something wrong, are they gonna value more this armed robber's opinion than my integrity?" And I think that that's when the low points come in almost every police officer's career. When you have your peers sort of judging you on something that you know is not true. So that bothered me more than, up to that point, a lot of things had bothered me. . . . When your superiors in the department doubt you for one minute, that sometimes causes you to lose some of the air in your sail. Because you know what you did was a good thing, you know what you did was an honest thing. You know that you know you would never do something [dishonest].

* * *

B5: I thought, "Why is it like this? Why should you have to go home and have to worry about the false claims of somebody you obviously locked up for valid and just reasons? Why should that hold any weight against your character?" I know that there is a process, and I don't want to say that we can let police officers do whatever they want. A lot of police officers will tell you this. I'm out there risking my life protecting the public, you know, facing dangerous situations many times, and this is what I get. I get a letter that says I stole something. It kind of amplifies itself. I don't think it's just me, 'cause I've heard other people's reactions to it and maybe that influenced the way I dealt with it. But I remember going home and thinking, you know, I'm a police officer, how can I steal? How can anybody accuse me of stealing? Why don't they see all the good things? And again, this is probably true in everybody's life, you always say, what about all the good things I do?

* * *

B5: You go through that period where you think, some day that's public record. That's public record whether it's true or not, it's there, and anytime that my character comes into question in the future, someone will have a piece of paper in there that says, "Weren't you accused of this?" That's all the public needs to hear. That's all, you know, a jury that's making a decision on your character needs to hear. It's that doubt. That reasonable doubt that we go by.

* * *

B5: I think, you know, somebody would of said this officer called me a name, he yelled at me and called me a name, I could handle that, that I could deal with.
I: But it's the implication of dishonesty.
B5: The implication that somebody is accusing [me] of doing something I put people in jail for.

Race and Gender Relations

I have noted in chapter 1 that policing is an occupation that has moved in a short time from being White male dominated to becoming a profession hospitable to women and officers of other ethnicities. According to officers, this transition has sometimes been a source of conflict and tension, which become manifest in group self-segregation, suspiciousness, mutual resentment, and difficulties in personal relations. This situation is destabilizing and creates discomfort and unease because of the obduracy of the problem and its unseemliness:

B16:   It is just not talked about because everybody is scared to talk about it. It's a big issue, and the young people look at it a lot differently than I do or than older guys do. And, in particular, a lot of the African American police officers, the young ones, have a really hard time adjusting to dealing with coworkers that are of the opposite color skin. It goes both ways, though. White people are the same way, but it is too bad. Because, like I said, when I came on this job, race wasn't even an issue —we were all friends; we all wore blue, and that is the way it was and nobody even mentioned it. There was none of that going on. . . .

Once you build up a wall, it's hard to break it down, but I've seen it. The wall gets higher on the race issue, instead of getting lower. You think that in the 90s that everybody would go, "Let's get along here; we are all on the same team," but it is not like that. . . . I mean, you got to depend on the guy sitting next to you with your life. You don't want to have any bad thoughts about him, or thinking negative things, especially on the color, on account of his race. I mean, that has nothing to do with how he is [as] a police officer. . . . You can feel it, you can feel it in the everyday work place. When you walk in a room, you feel it. If you walk in a room and there [are] five Black guys and all of sudden nobody is talking, you know what is up. And it's the same thing if you're a Black guy and you walk in a room and five White guys all shut up, then you know what is going on.

* * *

B18:   I am stuck here. I am really stuck, and then when they start joking with the ethnic jokes, you know: Look at that monkey or look at that, it's just that when your skin is cringing inside, and you're like, do you have to be like that? Why do you have to be like that? and, Who am I to try and change them? It's not that it's not worth it to me, it's just that I don't feel like that feminist is me. I am better off just to be quiet and go home and end the day.

* * *

B15:   They feel that they are over here and the rest of the department is over here. . . . There is a feeling that there is a difference in the administration with discipline; that there is a difference in the representation that is afforded to them by the union.

* * *

B7:   What you're going to have is a racial war in a precinct.
I: You think that it is getting close to that juncture?
B7:   This thing is heavy here. Yeah, it is so thick.
I: Strong feelings?
B7:   Strong feelings. It is so thick on both sides.

* * *

I: Would you say that there is any tension between males and females in this department? Any resentment on one side or the other?
B16:   Nobody, except for me.

* * *

B18:   Some females think that they have to have that bitch attitude and that vulgarity to let them know.
I: "I am police"?
B18:   Yeah, "I am the police. . . ." There are some women that I notice that feel that they have to prove themselves. They have to prove themselves worthy of the job or whatever or show their male partners that they can handle themselves. And they get that bitch name because people respect you more when you're a bitch. There are a lot of guys on the department that don't feel that this is a job where women belong. They just don't feel that

women should be police officers. . . .

A lot of the guys that I was in the academy with are like, you know, "Well, I didn't feel at first that it was a woman's job, but you all sweated it out and did the same things that I had to do through the academy, and you made it."

Management of Work Stress

Work-related stress and family-related stress are inherently interconnected, and a person who is stressed cannot easily compartmentalize himself or herself and separate one from the other. If a person has serious problems at home, the feelings of frustration that these problems generate are likely to affect the way he or she responds to situations at work. By the same token, bothersome and painful experiences on the job can leave resentments and undigested recollections that manifest themselves through irritability, moodiness, and un-communicativeness with significant others.

Where stress is exported or imported in this fashion, other people's responses to stress-motivated conduct at home or at work can create further stress, leaving the person feeling that he or she is being assaulted from all sides. Alternatively, the person may feel that other people are being insufficiently considerate of his or her stressed condition, despite a failure to reveal the nature of this condition. This cycle, as it relates to policing, is captured by the following description:

> B7:   You know, people go to sleep and they like to see beautiful dreams. But what if you were earlier that day part of a suicide where somebody just blew half themselves away, and you witnessed that? Now it is 9:00 p.m. and you have to lay your head down. What do you see when you close your eyes as a police officer? You have your mate next to you, be it male or female, she wants your attention, your sensitivity, your understanding. . . .
>
> She says she wants you to open up. She doesn't want to know that today you were on a homicide and the body you see is not like on television—the body was not just

lying there. This is a very hideous homicide. . . . So you try to keep it inside you, now you lay down, but what do you see, you know? You see that body still there, you got to suppress this within you. All of a sudden you find yourself spending time at the bar—that's when the drinking starts. You also find you surround yourself with other police officers because you're always talking about police scenarios.

Now you're at home. They find you a little edgy because the little trivial things that everybody is running around the house being all excited about, you're looking at them—"What is all that? That is nothing—you can't handle that?" So your wife, she says, "Well, I had a problem—the lights went out today." "So what? You can't handle that? I got to come home and deal with this? You understand what I just saw? I went to a house today and saw somebody hanging. I was in the middle of a big brawl, I saw somebody stabbed. I saw somebody run down the street that had just been shot with a shotgun on one half of his face. I come home and you're telling me that you're disturbed because you couldn't think of what to cook?" So now you have this agitation—your mate starts to pull away from you because you're not the same person that you once [were]. That is why you got to have those other outlets—because all of a sudden now it's 10:00 p.m. and she's wondering why you can't sleep.

"I had to deal with a dead baby and the mother. What is [it] that you want to tell me about *your* job?" But she is right—she has the right to tell you about her job because whatever happened on her job is dramatic and important to her. But see, you got to block out your part. You're saying, "Okay, let me get up and leave—I got to get out of here. I can't stay here because your problem to me on a scale of 1 to 10 is a minus 1." "But where are you going?" "Well, I'm going where the fellows are." When I get there, there's a couple of Molson Ice waiting for me.

Taking the Job Home

Some officers proclaim as a matter of inviolate principle that it is inappropriate to share stress-producing experiences with their spouses. One reason cited for this normative stance is that it is unfair to burden anyone with ugly and disturbing facts, especially when they have problems of their own. A related argument is that one must be protective and considerate of the sensibilities and delicate feelings of others— especially family members. A third argument is that civilians cannot visualize or understand police-related problems, and it is pointless to allude to events people cannot appreciate. A corollary of this argument is that one can discuss stress-producing experiences only with other officers:

> B11: I never bring my job home. No matter if it's good or bad. I never bring it home. . . . I mean, there are days where this job really gets to you. Certain things you see, certain things you have to do, where it really brings the stress out. Well, I don't go home and put the stress on other people. I just keep it inside of me, that's it. My wife, my kids, that is why I am working this job: to take care of them, not get them any kind of stress.

* * *

> B17: Well, I got three young kids at home, and I don't want them to see Daddy come and be miserable or be high-strung or upset about certain things. That is why I just leave it at work. It is a very impersonal note, but I look at it to where it is a job. I have a job to do. I do the job and when I am done with work, my job is over.

* * *

> B13: If it affects you personally and you take it home, it affects your family life, and that is no good. You have to separate the job from your family.

* * *

> B23: So if something happened that was humorous then, of course, I would tell her, but I would never tell her the other side.
> I: So just sort of the human interest stuff, that would sort of amuse her.
> B23: Yeah, break the ice.

* * *

B16:   I only tell my wife, she knows about funny things that happen, other than that I don't tell her about none of the body counts or any of the gruesome things that you actually see, because really unless you see it, you really can't comprehend it. You have to be there in order to really comprehend it, that is my feeling on it anyway. . . .

* * *

B19:   And it is so hard to explain to people that you go into other people's homes, and you see these things, and how upsetting they are. And no matter how hard you try to tell somebody—until you are actually there at 3:00 in the morning and it is pitch black and there are no lights on anywhere, no matter how hard you try to explain to somebody, until they would actually sit in the back of a police car and respond to a call, people just don't believe it. It is frustrating to try and get the point across sometimes.
I: With your husband do you have the feeling that he is hearing you but he can't quite get the gist of it?
B19:   Right, oh sure. That is why I think police officers [form] their own clique, because we have all done it. So when you explain it to another officer, they respond differently—like they are really involved in it—than when you talk to someone else, they are like, "yeah." So that is why I think a lot of people don't even bother—they just go to work and discuss these things.

Paradoxically, police officers who share an occasional stress-producing experience with their spouse find the disclosure helpful, but this does not lead them to conclude that work-related problems should be discussed at home.

I: You did say that you occasionally talk to your husband about things that happen at work.
B18:   Oh yeah. I talk to him a lot but, see, he is not a police officer. He doesn't know the atmosphere, he doesn't know, and he is kind of an easygoing guy, and I

will come home and tell him something if something is aggravating me or something, and then he will say, "Well, just do this," and I'll say, "It is not that easy, not that easy, you don't understand, I can't just do that." . . . then I'll shy off from telling him because I know what his answer is going to be. "Well, just tell her," or, "Just do this," or, "Just do that." If you don't know me by now, you know that it is not that easy for me to voice my. . .
I: What he is really saying is if he was in your shoes, he would do that. But he listens.
B18:   He does.
I: Do you find it helpful to vent a little bit with him?
B18:   Yes.
I: You do?
B18:   I do.

* * *

B16:   But I eventually did talk to her later on in the evening. So we went and did our family thing, and I got my mind off of it for a while, but later on when we laid in bed and stuff and she is going, "Is it something with me?" She started wondering if it was something with her and all that, she kind of pumped me, and then I broke down, and I had to tell somebody, I got to tell somebody, you know, I go and I told her the story and she goes, "Oh God, that's terrible." . . . And so I told her, and I did feel better after that, but we never talked about it again after that. And I am fine. I mean, it's just part of the job.

Dealing With One's Feelings at Work

Stress is initiated by a disequilibrating event, which results in feelings of distress. Police officers have special concerns relating to such feelings. Police are expected to be in control of events, which requires officers to appear cool, collected, businesslike, and dispassionate. However, an emotionally cold, robot-like, and aloof demeanor can be off-putting for civilians, who expect humane responses from those in authority. If an officer suppresses feelings to get on with the job, he or she must also deal with these undigested feelings in some fashion later. These are some of the occupational dilemmas experienced by officers when they face stressful encounters:

B5: The general public expects robots. Expects people with no emotions. They think that you just go in there and you're supposed to constantly be professional. And it's that whole thing about you shouldn't do this because you're a cop, or cops shouldn't behave this way, cops never lose their tempers, cops, you know, always are stern and strict and disciplined, and you know, don't get rattled. There are things that, you know, aggravate us in certain situations, that aggravate us and rip our emotions just like everybody else. When you see a kid hurt, I don't care who you are, it affects you. You do your job and you set your emotions aside, but you know that every cop after that goes home and sits down and deals with it. With what they saw and what they had to do. . . . As much as you learn with your training in the academy to be a professional and deal with it, it's tough. And then you see the family gathering around and the emotions start flying and you realize that no matter what happens, you know, this is what I have to be now. I have to be robotic and I have to go about this in a robotic fashion. . . . Then the reality sets in.

* * *

B14: Ninety-nine percent of the things that we go through, out on the street, is mind over matter. I am not going to get upset and react negatively because this lady doesn't agree that I'm telling her husband to get out, or he doesn't agree that he has to leave. I am going to sit there and take their abuse, and that is taking mind over matter. I am going to be called every [expletive] name in the book, and instead of acting negatively, I will just wait it out.

* * *

B17: While you're at the scene, you do what you have to do. When you're dealing with the family, you feel their loss and feel their suffering—but the point is, I turn it off.

I: Even there, you mean?
B17:   Not at the scene. At the scene I do what I have to do. If I am dealing with the family, I show them the respect during their time of grief, but once I leave the scene I turn it off.

* * *

B7:   When I go into somebody's house, generally, if I am going on a DOA or something like that, I'll be very respectful—they have just lost a loved one. I will usually ask them, "Do you mind if I say a prayer and a verse over your loved one?" And then I do something that probably nobody else will do. I give them the condolences of the city, the mayor, and the commissioner at this time. I still got to take an official report, but I don't have to go in there and be so bureaucratic, you know—"Yeah, let me see, okay."

* * *

B12:   It is unfortunate, I think, that I still have emotions like that. . . . But I still have these emotional feelings. You know, I think when it was getting to me, I says, "Well, now it's time for a change. I got to get out of here." . . . I just thought for me I had to leave, you know.
I: To keep your sanity.
B12:   Well, yeah, you know. Here I am supposed to deal with this stuff every day. But I mean, the hardest police officer would break down if they encounter something like that, I don't care how hard that copper thinks he is. You know, you see a child 5 years old that had something done to her. I mean, that is not natural.

* * *

B10:   And the low points just don't end that night, and you say, "Oh my God, that is terrible, see you later," you go home, and everything is hunky-dory. It don't work like that. You take it with you.

Beyond the challenge of husbanding feelings when they arise lie more long-term tasks, which have to do with preventing continuing distress and readjusting to familiar routine. The recovery process is exacerbated by the discontinuity between work and civilian life, especially if one wants to keep the former from intruding into the latter.

As some officers see it, they need to decompress when they leave work feeling tense or preoccupied, which calls for an interval of relaxation. If distress persists, officers resort to distracting activity, physical exercise, or a hobby:

> B23: Say I had a bad call, whatever the call was. Instead of going home like I usually go home, I would drive a longer way home.
> I: Until you cooled off.
> B23: Yeah, and then by the time I got home, then I was ready to go.
> I: Yeah, so what you are talking about is sort of a decompression period?
> B23: Yeah, you have to have that.

* * *

> B18: You need a winding-down period, especially if you had a stressful day. Especially if you have had like 40 calls and, you know, they were all high-incident calls, not fun ones, or you know, blow-off ones. You definitely have to take a few minutes.

* * *

> B17: It is just the way that I approach this, and I've seen a lot of coppers that would take the job home with them and be miserable and upset, and a lot of coppers take the job and go to the bar, and I just didn't want to do that. . . . If I feel that I can't handle something like that, very emotional, something happened at work and you are emotional to that point, I will go somewhere to relax me and then go home.

* * *

> B12: And you know, you try to work around that problem. If you got a project to do at home, you try to immerse yourself in that. [But] it will always haunt you no matter what. There are cases that I remember, and I

haven't worked back there in 7 years, $7^1/_2$ years, and there are still cases that are in my head; they are just still there. I mean, if I dwell on it.

I: You mean the images sort of come in and then you try to push them back down?

B12: Oh sure. Sure, there's one where a child wound up brain dead, all right? The child was in the hospital for a year, and then the child finally died, and you see X-rays of the spinal column and all that. How it's twisted. And you know, you just see these things, so you keep it down or you don't bring it to the family's attention. If you're alone, it comes up, you try to deal with it the best you can. I can't speak for everybody else. You know, I am sure some people might break down. Some people might, like I say, find a project to work on and just try to get it back out of their mind.

I: But you pick up a bunch of nails and a hammer and . . .

B12: Yeah, if I can't fix something, I'll sure as hell break it. . . . These are just some things that you learn to live with, and these are images that I am going to live with the rest of my life. That's just part of my job.

Management of Lingering Work Stress

Lingering or persisting distress affects a person in a variety of ways—all of them undesirable. The most direct impact includes symptoms of depression, such as insomnia and inability to concentrate. There are also indirect ways in which a person's health can be impaired, because stress overloads emergency measures that the body takes to deal with challenges and emergencies.

Most visibly, stress manifests itself through inappropriate behavior—responses to other people that are not entirely rational because they are contaminated by strong feelings. Such conduct reduces the quality of a person's contribution in jobs that involve other people, as most jobs do. In extreme cases, a stressed person can become a liability to his or her employers. Organizations in which stress is prevalent can have productivity problems related to sloppiness, tardiness, and absenteeism at work.

But stress does not need to show up as a direct or neat chain of cause and consequence. One reason is that efforts to reduce distress can backfire and do more harm than good. Most obvious is the matter of drinking, discussed (and deplored) by officers. Alcohol is a depressant; it can ameliorate pain and facilitate catharsis. But these modest gains can be overshadowed by enormous liabilities, especially for people who are predisposed to alcohol addiction.

A different unfortunate response to distress is retreat into self-insularity. This type of behavior can be misunderstood in relationships, even where one's significant others are indulgent, sensitive, and undemanding. Self-insulation is also apt to increase a person's despondency, because it invites escalating ruminations and the husbanding of grievances.

Emotional escalation can simultaneously be socially facilitated. Alienation at work can take the form of "gripe sessions" in which unhappy people exchange notes about their grievances, reinforcing each other's disgruntlement and resentment.

Officers who encounter stressors and residual feelings of distress face elements of all these hazards. In police work, the norm of "not taking the job home" forecloses a set of opportunities for sharing grievances and gaining support; the premise that revealing one's feelings is unprofessional reduces another opportunity. Peer support and solidarity can be helpful, but locker room cliques encourage the pooling of vexation. Post-shift constabulary libations—the hallowed police tradition of meeting at the bar after work—can serve the same problematic ends.

Our interviews did not suggest that stress is an endemic problem for officers. They instead indicate that officers very frequently feel that they have a clear idea as to what the stress problem is and are prepared to somehow address it. Our excerpts document the fact that officers can be insightful, self-aware, and self-analytic. Some of the officers, at least, are attuned to the origins of their distress and to its consequences, especially in relation to critical-incident stress (see chapter 8). They do not deny or distort their own vulnerability, humaneness, and fellow feelings, nor do they minimize the resentments that are rooted in a sense of injustice, evoked by prevailing perceptions of organizational inequity.

In summary, no one really needs to educate the officers about the problem of police stress or to sensitize them to the risks that it may pose. Most of the officers know that their work exposes them to situations that are potentially traumatizing. They know that their jobs can invite problems at home, and that their family problems can intrude on their work. They know that unfeeling or ritualistic organizational practices can be annoying and that conflicts with work associates can be disruptive. The officers assume that policing can be a stressful occupation, although they primarily regard their jobs as exciting, fulfilling, and satisfying.

3

Occupational Stress

Concurrent with the interviews excerpted in chapter 2 we ran a set of eight focus groups. We also engaged in informal "ride-alongs," which are described in chapter 4. The focus groups were designed to facilitate designing a survey by centering on the definition of stress. This chapter relates what these groups had to say about the nature of police department and family-related stress. It then reviews what the surveys suggested about the intensity and prevalence of occupational stress.

Focus groups happen to lend themselves to the surfacing of dissatisfactions. On their own—given the right subject—they verge on ebullient gripe sessions in which discontents can be shared and explored and sometimes even socially reinforced. In this sense, focus groups stand in contrast to more intimate interviews, which can facilitate the expression of privately held, and sometimes unpopular, views.

In our focus groups, we added balance by asking, "What do you like about your job?" before we asked, "What do you not like about your job?" Predictably, the latter type of responses took vehement center stage, although in seven of eight groups, the officers started by describing police work in familiar, glowing terms; in fact, the coordinator of the focus groups went so far as to report that "basically, these officers enjoy police work." He noted that group members had declared that they liked working with people, they enjoyed helping people, and they prized having a job that offered the chance to seek out such experiences. The officers contended, he wrote, that "the variety of work and encounters with different people and tasks make the officer's job satisfying."

One officer in one group emphasized that he appreciated seeing bad people convicted, and others also mentioned "good arrests" as sources of satisfaction. But most of the members of the groups traced any sense of accomplishment they experienced to opportunities for assisting crime victims and ordinary citizens.

The police job was described as "fun" and "not like work." One officer said of himself that he was an "adrenaline junkie." Another officer explained, "One moment there is an armed robbery, and the next minute you could be delivering a baby. Catching bad guys one minute, and giving a ride to someone who has no gas the next." A third officer said, "You never know what is going to happen, [and] every unknown factor is exhilarating." Having relative autonomy was described as part of the enjoyment. Autonomy meant that one's job "is what you make of it," that, as one officer put it, "I do what I want to do."

Sources of Stress Cited in Focus Groups

The officers deemed some citizens more deserving than others and saw many members of the community as hostile or vociferously unappreciative. But they suggested that citizens' complaints were less annoying than the reactions of administrators, who accorded these complaints more credibility than they deserved (officers in some of the groups also alluded to bad police work they felt was too leniently dealt with by their department).

The Department as a Stressor

In general, the theme of the sessions became the assertion that the prime stressors in policing are police administrators.

According to the group coordinator, administrators were seen as conduits of "politics," defined as encompassing interference from outside the department and "old-boy" networks inside the department. Group members repeatedly asserted that good performance in policing is not rewarded and that promotions are based on favoritism. A group reporter wrote that "political problems seemed to be narrowed down to promotional and policy concerns. The best person may not get a job because (another has) a political connection. . . ." The majority of officers felt that promotions were often unrelated to merit or achievement. The focus groups expressed an overwhelming feeling of "it's *who* you know, not *what* you know."

Many examples were cited involving unsuccessful meritorious candidates for promotion and successful nonmeritorious ones. Other examples had to do with inequitable disciplinary dispositions. One group reporter noted that "[there is a] belief that complaints against some officers [are] not investigated seriously." When the topic of behavior standards was raised in another group, the reporter noted, "Ugh! Immediate grunts from the entire group." Disciplinary actions were characterized as "a source of more stress than the whole job." One officer said that "the call of duty is *not* stress. Robbery, fighting, and so forth are part of the job. The worst stress comes from lack of respect and neglect."

Another area of concern was labeled "communication." A supervisor said that "the troops want consistency" but that "rules get changed everyday." There was reference to "roadblocks" and "red tape" that prevented things from getting done. One group member argued that "communication should flow bottom up and within as well." Failures to be fully informed were cited as a frequently recurrent problem: "There may be a shooting in the district next to you, but the information is not passed on. The problem may end up in your area, but you won't know."

The leadership of police departments was described as too distant and insufficiently concerned with the problems of the rank-and-file officers. Police administration was described as having "lost touch with the line." As one officer put it, "they have no clue on what it is like to be on the streets." However, negative feelings were tinged with ambivalence; the consensus was that with backing from the top, organizational improvements could be made, and that some changes could make the job easier and the work more effective.

Stress and the Family

In the interviews (see chapter 2), the officers sometimes asserted that they made a point of "not bringing the job home." In the same vein, the coordinator of the focus groups reported that "officers generally said that they did not talk about job-related problems with [their] family or significant others."

But officers voiced varying convictions about appropriate work-related discourse. One officer admitted that he "vents" to his family; another said he "talks" but not "bereaves"; he said he introduced work experiences as "an 'oh, by the way,' thing," thus making light of stressful encounters. A third officer reported that he made a special point of sharing "the good and the bad." A fourth asserted that "belaboring an issue can make you depressed." Another officer noted that "he didn't talk" to his wife and, as a result, "that marriage dissolved." He "now talks" to his second wife, and "she is interested." By contrast, a sixth officer said he initially told his family "everything—traumas [included]," but over time had evolved a policy of telling them increasingly less. Another said that his girlfriend—a lawyer—brought humor to bear on "ridiculous" experiences, placing them in perspective. Some officers said they were married to fellow officers, making it very difficult to separate shop and pillow talk. And several officers credited their family life with stress-reducing capabilities.

Family stress is discussed in more detail in chapter 4. In the focus groups, policing was described as an asset and a liability to one's family. On the one hand, policing can be seen as a prestigious and glamorous occupation, a source of pride to family members. One officer said that he took his wife on ride-alongs; another "took his children to cells and put them in, to show them what it is like, as a teaching mechanism." He also let them " 'shoot' his gun and took them out in his squad car." (The same officer, paradoxically, said he never talked about police work.) A third officer declared that his work gave him an edge as a father. As a result of his experiences with criminals, his children "know how to act, where they stand—know he will not put up with [misbehavior]."

The liability of policing to families can be stigmatization and problems related to shift work. The children of officers can also sometimes be singled out, labeled, and subjected to peer pressure. Civilians who discover that someone is a police officer will often turn the subject of conversation to personal gripes about police matters such as parking tickets, so that officers find socializing with other officers an inviting alternative.

Ameliorating Stress

Group members postulated that police stress must be dealt with because it is inevitable. Several officers emphasized the need for meaningful involvements and distractions. Examples of outlets that were mentioned in the groups included hunting, skiing, tennis, golf, traveling, snow mobiling, sponsoring sports teams, working with youths, remodeling one's home, wood carving, weight lifting, scuba diving, walking one's dog, mowing the lawn, watching television, and going to movies. Playing with one's children was a powerful relaxant for some officers, but others said that "children are more stressful than the job."

Alcohol use for "self-medication" was cited as an ever-looming danger. One officer ascribed his heart attack (at age 42) to drinking and proclaimed that he no longer drinks. Another recalled an embarrassing alcoholic partner. The officers as a group agreed that in the past, supervisors "used to cover for drunk cops," but that "the department (now) does not tolerate blatant drunks."

The officers in the groups agreed that there was a clear need for stress-reducing assistance but that there were equally clear reasons for being cautious. Peer counseling (e.g., Alcoholics Anonymous meetings) was seen to have advantages, because "one can relate to other officers." But whereas peer counselors "could be subpoenaed in lawsuits," professionals tended not to understand police work. Ideally, "an officer with a psychiatry degree" would be a person "to talk to that recognizes the problems, but with a degree to explain them." As for employee assistance programs, a group reporter noted that officers "did not trust it; were afraid of leaks, breaches of confidentiality, fear of being labeled (drugs, crazy, etc.)."

Some group members suggested a police-sponsored day care center staffed with people "you can trust to watch kids." One of several female officers said the departments would benefit from such facilities because "the worry of kids' care makes it difficult to concentrate on work."

What officers under stress were said to need were "retreats," support, peer counseling and assistance, and help with family problems. Police executives—who were most frequently regarded as uncaring—were challenged to demonstrate that they do care by sponsoring such arrangements.

Planning the Surveys

In our first planning session, the coordinator of our focus groups relayed an unsparing summary of group deliberations, including a recitation of reservations that had been expressed about the departments' administration. The summary was discussed with surprising delicacy, honesty, and candor, because the commissioner of the city department was present as a member of the planning group.

The coordinator's report was received without the slightest indication of strain or discomfort. Where tension did surface —in our second planning meeting—it reflected a derivative concern about whether the inquiry that was being formulated (especially with out-of-town academics involved) could in fact be a dispassionate one. A retired officer, who had been added to the group, voiced the suspicion that substantial issues would not be addressed in the survey. A second group member opined that the outcome of the survey was preordained. Both officers resigned from the project. A third officer also announced that he might resign if union understandings were violated.

These resistances and tensions surfaced as the group's task shifted from the delineation of areas to be covered in the survey to a definition of subjects to be embodied in questions. The difficulty of writing survey questions was undoubtedly one source of discomfiture. But the nature of the controversial subjects to be covered was presumptively another factor. Although the survey was to be a comprehensive one, the group was aware that the results could highlight focus group resentments about the way the police departments were administered. Some members were presumably fearful that the instrument could be tailored to downplay such organization-related concerns and to distort or underrepresent the feelings of officers.

The instrument that emerged (see Appendix B) was in fact a compendium of questions drafted by the planning group itself under rubrics that matched the subjects raised in focus groups, as well as those reported by the observer who had participated in ride-alongs. This observer had gathered impressions (which are discussed in chapter 4) about concerns of female and ethnic minority officers.

Occupational Stress as Defined in the Survey

The letter accompanying the stress survey (see Appendix A) defined *stress* as "feelings of emotional strain, pressure, discomfort, anger, uneasiness, and/or tension." The first question the survey asked the respondents was, "Would you say that you are experiencing some work-related discomfort or stress?" In answer to this question, 15.6% of the city sample and 9.6% of the suburban sample indicated that they experienced "a great deal" of discomfort or stress (see Appendix C). Six of 10 officers reported that they felt at least some stress. This is not an inconsiderable level of stress, but it is arguably moderate.

In identifying the sources of experienced discomfiture, both samples of officers highlighted organization-related grievances (Table 3.1). The three areas that were most frequently classed as "very stressful" were, unsurprisingly, those of internal departmental politics, the department's leadership, and inadequate information. These areas were the salient concerns highlighted in the focus groups. The next most frequently cited source of high stress was "witnessing child abuse," which was a subject that had prominently surfaced in interviews. Lowest ranking were difficulties in the community, violence, and "the impact of the job on my fam-

Table 3.1

Officers' Highest Ranking Sources of Stress in the Two Police Departments

Source/Rank	% in urban department ($N = 269$)	% in suburban department ($N = 104$)
Internal departmental politics		
Very stressful	34.9	40.4
Stressful	35.3	43.3
Not stressful	15.6	14.4
No response	14.1	1.9
The department's leadership		
Very stressful	35.3	49.0
Stressful	30.9	36.5
Not stressful	19.3	12.5
No response	14.5	1.9
Inadequate information		
Very stressful	31.2	23.1
Stressful	39.4	46.2
Not stressful	20.4	28.8
No response	8.9	1.8
Witnessing child abuse		
Very stressful	26.0	26.0
Stressful	36.1	34.5
Not stressful	17.8	37.5
No response	20.1	1.9

ily." Supervision by immediate supervisors and the adequacy of the reward system also ranked relatively low as concerns (Table 3.2).

The emphasis on administrative grievances in defining occupational stress emerges elsewhere in the survey (Table 3.3). In answer to the question, "Do you think that your level of motivation or commitment has been diminished by any actions of the Department's administration?" four of ten city

Table 3.2

Officers' Other Sources of Stress in the Two Police Departments

Source/Rank	% in urban department (N = 269)	% in suburban department (N = 104)
Problems in the community		
Very stressful	14.5	1.9
Stressful	40.1	31.7
Not stressful	34.6	61.5
No response	14.1	4.0
Experiencing violence		
Very stressful	8.2	2.9
Stressful	34.9	31.7
Not stressful	43.9	63.5
No response	13.0	1.9
Impact of the job on family		
Very stressful	10.0	3.8
Stressful	31.2	46.2
Not stressful	34.6	47.1
No response	24.2	2.9
Quality of immediate supervision		
Very stressful	12.3	16.3
Stressful	23.8	28.8
Not stressful	44.2	52.9
No response	21.9	8.9
Inadequate reward or recognition		
Very stressful	13.4	9.6
Stressful	29.7	29.8
Not stressful	46.8	54.8
No response	10.0	5.8

Table 3.3

Officers' Other Occupation-Related Responses in the Two Police Departments

Question/Response	% in urban department (N = 269)	% in suburban department (N = 104)
Do you think that your level of motivation or commitment has been diminished by any actions of the Department's administration?		
Often	39.8	49.0
Sometimes	30.9	31.7
Very occasionally	15.6	12.5
Never	6.7	6.7
No response	7.0	0
Do you see any problem of fairness with the system of promotion within the Department?		
A great deal	40.9	43.3
Some	29.7	38.5
Very little	11.2	13.5
None	10.4	4.8
No response	7.8	0
To what extent do you think that external political pressures adversely affect the Department's effectiveness?		
A great deal	46.1	37.5
Some	37.5	46.2
Very little	6.7	12.5
None	2.2	2.9
No response	7.4	0

officers and half of the suburban respondents answered "often." (Only 6.7% of each sample responded "never.")

The same picture emerged with respect to the question, "Do you see any problems of fairness in the system for promotions within the Department?" Only 10% of city officers and 5% of suburban officers said there were no problems. An equivalently small minority (2%) of both departments replied

"None" to the question, "To what extent do you think that external political pressures adversely affect the Department's effectiveness?"

A substantial minority of respondents said they were currently experiencing at least some work-related stress. Most current work-related stress was reported by older, experienced, and male officers. Interestingly, there were no obvious differences in reported stress levels by race or by education.

Occasions for Stress

Table 3.4 summarizes some of the problems that the city officers identified as sources of personal stress in open-ended responses. Experiences relating to death or injury make up much of this list. This was a subject brought up in interviews but not raised in the focus groups. The shooting of a fellow officer (a recent event in the department) was most fre-

Table 3.4

City Officers' Personal Experiences Cited as Sources of Serious Work-Related Stress

Personal experience	# of responses
Being unfairly accused; unfairly dealt with when accused; being sued, complained against	21
Shooting a fellow officer; officer's death	17
Problem with a supervisor; having a problem supervisor	16
Problems with fellow officers; inefficient fellow officers	13
Injury or death of a child	21
Death, injury, violence (other)	11
Problems with assignment; unfair assignment	11
Involvement in a shooting	9
Having an undesirable partner	7
Workload	6
Insomnia and other stress symptoms	6
Other	17

quently mentioned as stressful. Witnessing the death or injury of a child was also repeatedly cited as a stressful experience, as in the following:

> The death of a child had a great impact on me.
> Recovery of a 10-year-old drowning victim.
> After investigating child abuse death and a horrific scene of violence.
> Murder of a young girl.
> An 8-year-old child [died] while I tried to revive her.
> Neglected children kept in home to hide bruises and malnutrition.

One of the officers provided added detail. He recalled, "While a rookie officer, I experienced a horrible death of a person. I became physically ill for approximately one month."

The next most frequently cited stressors related to unfair accusations, complaints, litigation, and treatment by the department:

> My partner and I got blamed for something that wasn't true. We were tried and convicted before we were even aware a complaint was made against us.

> When I acted in good faith, I had the stress of departmental evaluation of my actions.

> Sometimes, very bad things happen "on the street" and you could be sued or worse, and until they are over, you sometimes sweat blood.

> The officer is guilty until proven innocent rather than the other way around.

> Have been the target of criminal investigation and grand jury action based on allegations of persons I have arrested.

> Was indicted on a DA's witch hunt and had to go through a criminal trial—was acquitted—almost 20 years ago.

> In-house problems, where the administration is trying to nail you to the wall, and you feel they are stepping out of bounds.

Problems with supervisors and fellow officers (including partners) were also frequently mentioned as stressors. Examples of supervision-related complaints include the following:

> Two years ago I had a supervisor who had a personal grudge against me.
>
> No one recognized my efforts because the boss doesn't care for me personally.
>
> A lieutenant who constantly harassed me because of personality conflict—not because of any work-related conflict.
>
> Supervisors that had personality disorders.
>
> When a new patrol officer in the 80s, older lieutenant felt we should not be in the patrol force, so every tour (double back then) I had to walk a beat with little relief in the winter.

Examples of complaints relating to partners and fellow officers include the following:

> I have little faith in many of my fellow officers to properly do their job.
>
> I worked with an idiot.
>
> Coworkers who are lazy do-nothings.
>
> Shortly after I was hired I had to work with a partner who, if I had the opportunity, I would not have worked with.
>
> Early in my career, working with officers who were not committed and were not interested in teaching me the job.
>
> I don't get along with some of my coworkers.

Peer-related complaints centered on issues of effectiveness, integrity, or competence or on having to work with individuals who proved personally uncongenial.

Differences between the open-ended responses and the answers to more structured questions illustrate that the former can be useful in highlighting multidimensionality by adding nuances and variations to themes explored in a survey. Summaries of quantitative survey results provided an overwhelmingly monothematic picture of occupational stress. The heavy majority of respondents defined their department's leadership as a stressor. The majority, in fact, claimed that their commitment to the job had been diminished by "actions of the administration." Almost all respondents opined that "external forces" had adversely affected departmental policy.

When we asked the officers for experiences they could point to as sources of personal stress, they nominated a more diversified set of impingements. They also added connotations to administration-related grievances. Among these connotations, the most prominent were issues of fairness and equity. The most prominent concerns were with administrative actions that were seen as arbitrary and capricious or as insufficiently supportive of officers—especially when their careers were on the line. Thinking about experiences that are stressful invited nomination of critical incidents as sources of stress. It also evoked discussion of peer-performance issues, which was not a subject that our planning group had tapped with survey questions.

Similarities and Differences in the Responses

What is truly amazing, given the differences between the two departments, is that responses to most questions in the two surveys were virtually identical. Moreover, a few interesting differences resulted from contrasts between the city and suburban environments.

"Problems in the community" were adjudged "very stressful" by 15% of the city officers and 2% of suburban officers. "Media coverage" proved "very disruptive" to 31% of the city officers and 4% of suburban respondents. "External political influence" was less of a stressor in the suburban department, as was "fairness . . . related to race or gender."

Almost all (91%) officers in the suburban department—solidly comprised of White men—opined that "enough" or "too much" attention had been paid to issues of race and gender. Most of the suburban officers also declared themselves stressed by their department's leadership and asserted that their "motivation and commitment" had been "diminished" by administrative actions.[1]

Differences emerged with respect to strategies used by the officers to deal with work-related stress. Two-thirds of the suburban respondents reported that they physically exercised when stressed or engaged in some activity or hobby. By contrast, 41% of city officers and 18% of suburban officers said they had recourse to church or prayer. Forty percent of city respondents but 25% of the suburban respondents confessed to drinking alcohol to relieve stress. To a separate question, more than half (54%) of the suburban officers and more than a third (35%) of the city officers answered that they never used alcohol to deal with stress or tension, but 10% of the city officers said that they did so "often." Last, more city officers than suburban officers reported experiencing "nightmares or painful memories."

In answer to another question, two-thirds of both officer groups indicated that they discussed "work-related concerns or problems" with spouses or significant others, and half of both groups said that they shared problems with partners, other officers, or friends. Only 10% said that they kept their problems to themselves. This fact is of particular interest because it illustrates one result of a multipronged research strategy—that of apparent discrepancies in the emphasis of responses. Should we conclude that officers share experiences

---

[1] The suburban officers mentioned excessive workload and failure to be promoted among sources of stress. They also indicated that work-related stressors often act cumulatively. However, they did concur with the city officers in citing exposure to death or injuries and unfair accusations as sources of stress.

with their spouses (as they tell us in the survey), or that they "never bring the job home," as they claim in interviews? One answer is that both versions may be correct, depending on the content of the communication the respondents alluded to.

Sources of Occupational Stress

It is noteworthy that not only did officers in the two departments agree about what they regarded as stressful, but the stressors they identified coincide markedly with those cited in other studies. In their recent review, for example, Finn and Tomz (1997) listed the following as among "the most common sources of stress":

- unproductive management styles
- inconsistent discipline and enforcement of rules
- equipment deficiencies and shortages
- perceived excessive or unnecessary paperwork
- perceived favoritism by administrators regarding assignments and promotions
- lack of input into policy and decision making
- second-guessing of officers' actions and lack of administrative support
- inconsistent or arbitrary internal disciplinary procedures and review
- lack of career development opportunities (and perceived unfairness of affirmative action) with resulting competition among officers, especially in small departments, for the few available openings
- lack of adequate training or supervision
- lack of reward and recognition for good work. (p. 7)

Crank and Caldero (1991) studied mid-sized police agencies and reported that "it became increasingly apparent . . . that supervisors within the department were perceived to be a principal source of stress" (pp. 341–342). In particular, "upper management personnel were the most frequently selected single source of stress" (p. 343). One sample characterization of management was that "these heroic knights of the coffee cup are so lacking in any real creative intelligence as to be truly amusing, were it not for their indolence and inefficiency." In reviewing such highlights, Crank and Caldero pointed out that they were "tapping an unexpectedly intense reservoir of grievances" and concluded that

> Concerns over equitable treatment in assignments and promotions, malicious and self-protective behavior by supervisors, ambiguous policies and rules, and fears of internal review and investigation describe a complex web of organizational stress from which there appears to be no relief within the occupation of policing. (p. 347)

Souryal (1981) also noted the magnitude of the resentment and wrote that "officers are increasingly ranking the brass and the bureaucracy, along with the criminals, on their enemies list" (p. 60). A recent survey conducted in Los Angeles (Sterngold, 2000) produced the finding that "a majority of officers said that the best way to improve morale would be to remove [the chief of the police department]." The majority of officers in this survey also reported "they did not believe the department's management was honest or had integrity" and that it "systematically ignores their views and interests."

One of the most cogent analyses of this problem was that provided more than two decades ago by Martin Reiser (1974), a psychologist with the Los Angeles Police Department. He pointed out that police departments have the feel of an intimate patriarchal family, "with all the consonant feelings related to power, dependency, and independence" (p. 156). The intensity of rank-and-file resentments relating to the departmental hierarchy would thus be a result of the familial context in which the authoritarian practices of police administrators are experienced. Reiser wrote that

> Traditionally, the chief is all-powerful and rules with an iron, if not despotic, hand. The "brass" are usually older,

more powerful "siblings" who behave in a paternal and patronizing way toward the young street policemen who occupy the role of younger siblings striving and competing for recognition, acceptance, and adulthood. This dynamic profoundly influences the organization in many significant areas such as communication, morale, discipline, and professionalism. (p. 156)

Reiser also pointed out that management practices in police departments are notoriously anachronistic, in that they place heavy emphasis on control and monitoring of behavior and on the use of rewards and punishments as motivators. He wrote that

typically, the jackass fallacy is operative. This is based on the carrot and stick approach to personnel management, which assumes that without either dangling a tasty reward in front of someone's nose or beating him with a stick, he will not move. (p. 157)

This system is not designed to inspire quality productivity, but it does invite resentments about the fairness with which rewards and punishments are allocated. Reiser noted, for example, that "policemen tend to be very competitive, and failure of promotion at an anticipated time may result in feelings of alienation from the group, depression and low self-esteem" (p. 157).

Given findings such as these, it is noteworthy that stress-related interventions are largely "person-centered" (Bureau of Justice Assistance, 1990), leaving contextual sources of stress unaddressed. The problem to date is that "organizational reform . . . seems to have taken a back seat to other alternatives, even though there is considerable evidence from the organizational literature that more participatory styles of organization and leadership produce greater worker satisfaction" (Terry, 1981, p. 72). This issue is discussed later in chapters 6 and 9.

4

Gender, Age, and Family Stress

In 1968, two female police officers in Indianapolis were as-signed to patrol together. This was a pivotal moment in the history of women in policing. Women had now moved out of the station house and into the street, sharing the patrol duties that until then had been performed by male police officers (Schulz, 1995). However, male police officers and police administrators did not receive the idea of women on patrol with enthusiasm.

Until the 1960s, women had generally performed limited duties as police officers. They had done the jobs that were considered "women's work": dealing with other women and juveniles. Such restriction of women's participation in police work also occurred in the British police service, where after World War II, women continued to work in a separate "women's department," even though their duties were expanded to include driving and criminal investigation (Brown & Campbell, 1994). When women began to ride in patrol cars and to walk beats, they were assuming duties that had been defined as "men's work" or "real" police work (Hale & Wyland, 1993; Martin, 1980; Schulz, 1995; Segrave, 1995).

The first part of this chapter was written by Dr. Frankie Y. Bailey.

The resistance of male officers and administrators to women on patrol took a variety of forms. Women were not hired in significant numbers until the Equal Employment Opportunity Act of 1972 (P.L. 92-261) extended the Civil Rights Act of 1964 to state and local governments.[1] Even when women were hired and placed on patrol, their male colleagues continued to question whether they could do the job. Could they be depended on to provide adequate backup? Would they require protection by male officers? Were they physically and mentally able to cope with the demands of being a street cop? A number of studies (e.g., Martin, 1980; Sherman, 1975) were undertaken to determine whether women could perform the duties of a patrol officer. These studies examined the performance of women on patrol and concluded that women were able to do the job.

However, this research did not guarantee the acceptance of women into police departments. In fact, women continued to report that they were the targets of hostility from their coworkers and supervisors. They continued to report behaviors ranging from pranks and verbal abuse to sexual harassment and even sexual assault (e.g., Segrave, 1995). The lawsuits brought by women against police departments across the United States offered a picture of hostile workplaces in which women have been (and sometimes still are) excluded from the police subculture and treated as outsiders.

The coping strategies adopted by women as they enter a formerly male work environment have been examined by a number of scholars. One of the questions has been whether women as they are socialized into police work will adopt the

---

[1]However, the percentage of women in policing remains low relative to their percentage of the population. In 1986, they were 8.8% of police officers in cities with populations greater than 50,000 (Martin, 1980). Greene (1997) found that Black women have made some progress in joining the ranks of police officers (especially in those cities with majority Black populations and Black mayors). However, Black women are still only 2.2% of all sworn officers in local police agencies, compared with White women, who are now 5.7% of the total number in such agencies (Reaves, 1996b, cited in Greene, 1997). Also see Schroedel, Frisch, Hallamore, Peterson, and Vanderhorst (1996) and Dantzer and Kubin (1998).

styles of policing of their male counterparts (Belknap & Shelley, 1992; Berg & Budnick, 1986; Lanier, 1996; Lersch, 1998; Wexler, 1985; Worden, 1993). These research findings indicate that in response to their status as members of an organization who are not totally accepted because of their gender, women have developed coping strategies aimed at lessening the impact of male hostility and creating spaces for themselves in which they can function as police officers. However, as Haarr and Morash (1999) noted, a complex relationship exists among gender, coping strategies, and other factors such as race.

With regard to the stress experienced by female police officers, there are obvious gender-related sources of stress such as sexual harassment and exclusion from the male-dominated police subculture. There are also other stressors that some scholars suggest are inherent in the role conflicts experienced by women who are not only police officers but also wives and mothers. For example, women as mothers traditionally have been the principal caregivers of their children. As wives, women have been expected to perform the majority of the duties associated with maintaining a household (Martin, 1980, pp. 199–202). These expectations often still exist, and the working wife and mother may experience both physical and psychological stress as she attempts to cope with the demands of her home life and her job. Such stressors are, of course, not unique to women. Male police officers also experience the conflicting demands of home and job. And there are some "workplace problems" that are experienced by all police officers. However, even when women do not report greater levels of work-related stress than men, they "face a unique, gender-related set of stressful circumstances" (Morash & Haarr, 1995, p. 133).

Given the status of women in policing, as we began to develop the survey instrument, we thought it would be useful to gather some preliminary information from female officers. As indicated in chapter 1, we had decided that in addition to focus groups and formal interviews, it would be useful to engage in field observation in the form of "ride-alongs," specifically with female officers.

Results From the Ride-Alongs

Ten ride-alongs were completed by the female member of the research team over several months. She attempted to cover precincts or districts across the city and to include one ride-along in the suburban area. The ride-alongs lasted 2–3 hours and were done on day and evening shifts. In the city department, the selection of the officers with whom the observer rode was made by the shift supervisor of the precinct or district. The request made to the police department was that the observer be allowed to ride with a female officer and her male or female partner.[2] In addition, we also had an opportunity to ride alone with two lieutenants (one male, one female) and to spend time at various station houses informally chatting with the officers. In the suburban department, there was only one female patrol officer. We joined her for a ride-along during her evening shift.

The intent of these ride-alongs was to allow us to observe women on patrol and at the same time to engage the officer and her partner in informal conversation about the job. If the officers had not been briefed about the stress project, we told them that the research was under way and that a survey was being prepared. However, this explanation was kept as succinct as possible. The observer indicated her desire to simply ride with the officers for a few hours as they went about their routine duties.

Generally (except in her rides with the two lieutenants and the patrol officer in the suburb), the observer sat in the back seat. Conversation took place through the glass partition separating the front seat from the back. We engaged the officers in casual conversation about the city, the police department, and the nature of their work. Basic background information was elicited (e.g., years on the force, length of partnership). However, because of the informality of these conversations, the observer endeavored to keep note-taking to a minimum.

---

[2]In terms of demographics, the officers on these ride-alongs were 14 women (9 Black, 5 White) and 5 men (3 Black, 2 White).

Following each ride, the observer returned to her hotel room and made log entries based on the key themes and phrases she had jotted down and on her recollection of the events that had occurred.

Typically, the officers—a few after an initial hesitation—tended to take the conversational ball and run with it. Once they began to talk, they seemed to want the observer to understand their job and how they felt about it. They pointed out the features of the areas they patrolled and discussed the people who lived in the neighborhoods.

The observer was allowed to join the officers as they responded to calls. This provided her with an opportunity to observe the interactions between officers and citizens. After returning to the vehicle, she sometimes asked questions about those interactions. On one occasion, she observed a robbery call that involved a high-speed response and the foot chase of a fleeing suspect. This call brought a multiple-car response and allowed the observer to raise questions with the officers about the stress involved in such calls.

During the conversations between the observer and the officers, several themes emerged that were later discussed by the members of the stress research project team. These themes included (a) the nature of the job and sources of job satisfaction or stress, (b) the city itself and the environment of the beat, (c) the characteristics of a good partner, (d) the responses of citizens and fellow police officers to women on patrol, (e) the effect of the job on personal life, and (f) the role of "politics" in the police department.

Nature of the Job

With regard to job satisfaction, autonomy emerged as an important and valued aspect of their work. Several women pointed to the contrast between the jobs they had done formerly in offices and the relative freedom that they enjoyed as police officers on patrol. The salary and benefits that they enjoyed as police officers were also mentioned as a source of job satisfaction. The female officers were specifically pleased with the 10-hour, 4-day work week in the department, which gave them more time in which to take care of personal matters. The women as a group favored the day rather than the evening shift. Several noted that this allowed them to be at home when their children were. However, several women also noted that the day shift was "slower" (less action) than the evening or night shifts. On some beats, in low-crime neighborhoods, the officers reported there was not a great deal to do. Hence, boredom became one possible stressor. But the officers also noted the unpredictability of the job—as illustrated by emergency calls that resulted in an adrenaline rush followed by the return to routine and the need to shift back down.

Environment of the Beat

Another factor that the municipal patrol officers (women and men) identified as a source of stress was the city itself. Several discussed (often with wry humor) the difficulties of being out on patrol during a snowy, icy, bitterly cold winter. Aside from having to drive in bad weather, there was the necessity of getting out of the car and standing outside while writing reports. As one officer (a male partner) pointed out, officers have to remove their gloves to write or to get to their weapon. A female officer commented on the hats that were necessary to keep the head warm but were not particularly comfortable.[3] When asked about their protective vests, the officers observed that they were hot and heavy in summer, but in the winter, they provided warmth. And after the recent shooting of two police officers (one officer killed, one wounded), most officers agreed on the necessity of wearing them.

The communities that the officers patrolled showed the effects of deindustrialization and urban blight. The officers pointed out the condemned houses and the litter in vacant

---

[3]Regarding the uniform, a female officer noted during a trip to the restroom that one of the minor irritations women faced was that a trip to the toilet required removal of the equipment (guns, cuffs, keys) worn around the waist.

lots. As several officers observed, it was depressing to spend a shift driving through such neighborhoods. As one officer pointed out that the police rarely received calls from the less blighted streets on their beat. Therefore, they spent much of their time in visually unpleasant settings. However, the officers also noted that many good people lived in these decaying neighborhoods. The officers recorded their own depression at seeing these people struggling against such odds.

Several of the officers pointed out locations where a crime had occurred or a crack house or other place of illegal activity had operated. In discussing crime scenes, one officer (a male partner) noted that one of the problems that officers sometimes encountered was controlling the scene when citizens wanted to see what was going on. He noted that the media were also sometimes an annoying presence at crime scenes.[4]

Qualities of a Good Partner

When the conversation turned to what one aspect of the job made the work easier and more pleasant, the officers (women and men) were unanimous: having a good partner. A good partner was one with whom one could establish rapport and who could be trusted not only to back one up, but not to get one into trouble. A good partner was one whose policing style was—if not identical to—at least complementary to one's own (also see Pugh, 1986).

When asked by the observer whether they would prefer to ride with a woman or a man, several women said another woman. As two female partners put it, male officers could be difficult to work with because of their "ego." Other female officers echoed their assertion that male officers often created problems with citizens by the aggressive style in which they attempted to take control of a situation. These women felt that male officers were more likely to become involved in a

---

[4]Several of the officers mentioned the somewhat problematic relationship between the city police department and the local media. They felt that the police had received generally negative coverage from local media.

physical encounter with citizens. Women, on the other hand, were more likely to try talking before taking aggressive physical action.

However, the majority of the female patrol officers agreed with the male officers who were asked about this, that it was the personality of the partner that was important. A good partner was one—female or male—with whom one could get along. As several officers noted, there was nothing worse than spending a shift—or days or months—with a partner who was hostile or uncommunicative. The officers who had experienced not having a permanent partner noted the stress created by coming to work and not knowing with whom one would be assigned to ride during that particular shift.

Citizen Response to Female Officers

In discussing partners, the observer asked how citizens responded to different partner combinations—female–female, male–female, Black–White. This question was prompted by the observation of two female partners that some citizens were still surprised when female officers responded to calls. When this question was raised, a veteran female officer[5] noted that citizens had become much more accustomed to seeing female officers than when she came on the job 17 years earlier. However, several of the female officers who had ridden or were then riding with male partners said that some citizens still assumed that the male officer was in charge and directed their questions and comments to him. Several of the Black female officers noted that citizens sometimes preferred talking to a White officer. One Black female officer with a White female partner reported (and her partner confirmed) that she had been verbally abused by Black citizens who saw her as a traitor and had called her names, including "bitch." She felt that some citizens did not see her as a "real cop" and preferred to speak to her White partner. However, other

---

[5]Time on the job for all patrol officers (female and male) with whom the observer rode ranged from 1¹/₂ to 17 years.

Black female officers thought that citizens responded to them as "cops" rather than as "Black cops." That is, many citizens saw all police officers as being the same and often viewed them in negative ways. Related to this, two Black female partners said that one source of stress for them was the rude and abusive behavior displayed toward citizens by some other police officers. They were concerned about how citizens viewed police officers and how police officers treated citizens.

Effects on Personal Life

As some of the police officers noted, their job could sometimes have a negative impact on their personal lives. Most of the female officers described efforts to separate their professional and personal lives. Several of the female officers were presently married to male officers and talked of the value of having a spouse who understood what they did for a living and the stresses involved. But two female partners who were not married to police officers wondered aloud about how one could get away from the job when married to another officer (see Elliot, Bingham, Nielsen, & Warner, 1986).

The partners and several other female officers indicated their desire to relax with family and friends. Most of the women said that they still socialized with the friends that they had before becoming police officers. But at least two others (and a male partner) mentioned that their occupation had created strain between themselves and some former associates. Several officers reported the comment that they had received from friends or acquaintances that they were "acting like a cop." One male officer discussed the dilemma of what to do if friends do something illegal in front of you. One Black female officer, who was single, discussed the difficulties of dating. She found herself encountering men who were either intimidated by her and her job or were so fascinated by her work that they wanted to talk about nothing else. Several of the women spoke of the "groupies" who hang around male officers, and one suggested there were male equivalents.

The female patrol officers said they did not spend a great deal of time engaged in off-duty socializing with other officers (with the exception of husbands). But, with regard to male–female relationships, the women (and a couple of the male partners) commented on the reactions of female (non-police) spouses to having their husbands ride with a woman. One officer related that she had once had a male partner with whom she worked well and who had become a good friend, but they had ended their partnership because he was going through a difficult time in his marriage, and she was concerned about how his wife perceived their partnership. Other women observed that, because one spends so much time with a partner, male–female partnerships have the potential for becoming something more. They agreed on the necessity of being aware of and dealing with this.

Politics

Finally, as in the focus groups, the conversation turned to politics in the police department. Every police officer the observer rode with mentioned politics in one form or another. The women and their male partners spoke of politics in different ways, defining it broadly to include discrimination as well as manipulations by city officials and interest groups within the police department. In general, they spoke of the stress created by politics. On one occasion, the officers pointed to the condition of their station house and the shortage and condition of vehicles in their mostly ethnic minority (and high-crime) precinct as compared to the resources made available to officers working in predominantly White, middle-class areas of the city.

Other officers discussed the politics of promotion and special assignments, arguing that favoritism, sometimes based on race or gender, played a role in some such decisions. They indicated that even with civil service regulations in place, there was still room for biased maneuvering within the bureaucracy of the department. Several Black officers noted that few Black people held command positions. One Black male officer pointed to the racial tension in the department and the lack of impact of the diversity training that officers received. Several women cited the difficulties experienced by some female lieutenants. In general, the officers seemed to agree that even when they had a good immediate supervisor—almost as important as a good partner—the politics coming from above often created a stressful work environment. The coping mechanism most of them said they adopted was to focus on their job and try to do it well. However, several Black officers reported that self-segregation was occurring within the department, with both White and Black officers choosing to work together not just as partners but on certain shifts or in certain precincts.

Summary of the Observer's Impressions

The observer was impressed that the women seemed to value their ability to shape and control their job. They seemed to value autonomy and the work environment that they could create within the space of their vehicle with a compatible partner. They did not express the concern the observer had anticipated about matters such as child care. Although the majority of the women had children, they had worked out arrangements with spouses or other relatives to provide for child care. They did not show great concern about the conflict between their roles as wives and police officers (although it should be noted that several of the women were divorced or never married). What the women did express concern about were the conflicts within the department that affected their work environment. Only one of the women—the officer in the suburban department—spoke extensively about hostile male coworkers. She who was the only female patrol officer (two women were lieutenants) in the department.[6] This officer had found her early career particularly stressful but had developed strategies for coping with the attitudes of her

---

[6]In this respect, this officer could be described as a "token" woman (with regard to percentage of the total population) in the department. See Wertsch (1998) on policewomen and tokenism.

coworkers. She was now married to a fellow officer and was finally permitted (after some resistance) to ride alone on patrol.

However, with regard to sexism, two Black female partners did mention a sexual discrimination suit that a female officer had recently won against the police department. One of these officers noted that she herself had been given a hard time by a former supervisor, but it was difficult for her to tell if it was because she was Black or because she was female. A White female officer mentioned the suit brought by a female trooper against the state police. This officer observed that the harassment of the trooper had obviously "gone over the top." But she wondered if in the beginning the trooper might not have been able to stop the harassment by "just giving it back to them."

The observer gained the impression that female officers with more years on the job seemed more comfortable in their role. They seemed to have a sense of "ownership" of the beat that they patrolled. This appeared to hold true particularly for two female community relations officers, who enjoyed unfettered opportunities to interact with citizens. The observer was impressed by the comment made by one female officer that one needed to be able to take care of oneself while on patrol (rather than calling too frequently on other cars for backup). Comfort on the beat seemed to be linked to a sense of autonomy and independence (and a sense of competence as a police officer).

The conversations the observer had with the officers suggested that the women had entered policing by a variety of paths. Several had friends or family members who were police officers and had been influenced by them to join the force. Others had come to policing after having spent time in college or earning a degree. Some had joined the force after working at other jobs. This raised a question in the observer's mind about the relationship between knowledge of policing as an occupation and relative ease of adjustment. Another question that occurred to the observer after one Black female officer mentioned that her brother was serving time in jail is whether other officers (both female and male) might have relatives or friends who had experienced the criminal justice system from the other side. She speculated about the stress (and perhaps ambivalence about the criminal justice system) such connections might create for these officers.

Directly related to this was the experience of riding with Black police officers and conversations with them about the high-crime, often predominantly ethnic minority, communities that many of them patrol. Their comments, including those of the two Black female officers who felt that some citizens were harassed by other police officers, suggested that perceived inequities in law enforcement might be a variegated source of stress for some officers of color. Having made the choice to become police officers, there might be costs to remaining on the job (see Alex, 1969; Hochstedler & Conley, 1986; Holdaway & Barron, 1997). Finally, the observer concluded that the experiences of female, ethnic minority police officers must be sorted out to understand the work lives of women who must deal with both race and gender issues (see Martin, 1994).

Interaction with these police officers suggested that although there are many sources of actual and potential stress that all police officers share (e.g., the feelings of personal mortality following the killing of a police officer), there are other sources of stress that remain more salient for women than for men.

Results From the Surveys

An enticing incentive for undertaking our study was the anticipation of solutions we could suggest for addressing the complaints and unmet needs of the female officers we expected to surface. Conversations during the ride-alongs appeared to confirm our expectation that female officers would experience more problems relating to the job and family than would male officers. Women complained about problems of acceptance, and some of their discussions turned to marital problems that involved male partners and less-than-trusting spouses.

As we reviewed our other initial inquiries, several preliminary indications looked promising. In the focus groups (but not in the ride-alongs), female officers had brought up difficulties with child care and one or two of them had complained about cavalier responses to their pregnancies. Our advisory group had predicted widespread interest among mothers in day care arrangements in the department.

Several allusions in the interviews also touched on family issues. One officer, for example, discussed an acrimonious divorce early in her career. A second officer described a husband who made it difficult for her to decompress after work by asking insensitive and patronizing questions. She delineated the problem as follows:

> B18:   You have to be a different person on the job, and it does take a few minutes when you get home. I just have to sit down and relax and let it all, like, pass and disappear for a minute, and think, "Okay, I am home now and I have to take care of my child, and I have to pick her up and hug her and love her and not be upset that I have to do it or something." I am a family person. I am a wife and a mother, and I try not to treat my husband like he is one of the people out on the street. I try not to start using the vulgar language that sometimes comes out when you are out on the street, and I try not to bring that home and act like that and boss him around like he is one of the dirtbags that are out on the street or something.
>
> But, that is a little hard. Sometimes you have a bad situation at work, out on the street you had a bad day, you had a lot of irritable people that you had to talk to and deal with and you just are at your wit's end. Like, "If I talk to one more stupid person or if one more person spits in my face today, I am just going to lose it," and then if my husband comes home and says, "Oh, the bed is not made," or "How come the dishes aren't done?" or "What have you done since you've been home?" or something like that, it takes a real lot to just bite my tongue and say it is not worth it and just try to talk it out calmly and say, "Look it, I have had a bad day. Can you just get off my back for a few minutes?"

I: And that's as calmly and collected as possible?
B18:   Right. Sometimes it doesn't come out that way. Sometimes it will escalate, just like a situation out on the street. It will start out calm and then the voices start to rise, and then it's like full-blown argument.

Another female officer recalled that she had missed a promotional examination—thereby decelerating her career—because she felt hesitant to leave a sick baby with a caretaker:

B19:   And when the exam time came, my son was very sick the night before, and we had to be up at 8 o'clock. I didn't go. He was sleeping on my stomach on the couch and it was like 6 in the morning and I was like, "Well, this was meant to be." I couldn't leave him, there was no way—I don't care if I wanted this job more than anything. I can't leave my son, and he is like "Mommy," and he is sick. I said, "Oh well." So everybody said, "Why didn't you just leave him with Dad?" and I couldn't. It was meant to be. . . . I like where I am, and I am satisfied. It's good and it's nice to go home and have the little guy.

The group of officers who constructed our survey instrument accorded prominent place to the family stress area. Among questions they drafted was one that anticipated personal difficulties officers might have making child care arrangements. The group expected widespread interest in supplementary daycare provisions.

Level of Family-Related Stress

Family problems achieved a respectable but moderate place among sources of stress highlighted in the survey. Impact of job on family ranked 15th (past) and 19th (current) among 21 sources of stress. To a separate question, however, 67% (close to 7 of 10 officers) answered that work-related stress had sometimes (or often) affected their family lives. Half (47%) of the respondents indicated that family-related stress had affected their work. Four of 10 officers claimed having had difficulties balancing job and family responsibilities, and 37% said that they were currently experiencing family-related problems.

The survey for the suburban police department yielded comparable data, although the officers reported more moderate (or less frequent) stress levels.

Gender and Family-Related Stress

Table 4.1 displays the answers of the male and female officers to questions relating to family stress. Without exception, the male officers reported *more* family-related problems and *greater* impact of such problems. For example, whereas only about a third of female officers claimed that family-related stress had affected their work, more than half of male officers said that their motivation or performance had sometimes (43%) or often (12%) been affected. One of five men indicated that work-related stress had often spilled over into their home lives, but only 1 of 20 women said that this had often been the case. More than half the men (52%) reported having had difficulties balancing job and family responsibilities, compared to 46% of the women; the proportions for frequent difficulties are 14% and 7%, respectively. The proportion of the men who said that they currently experienced "a great deal" of family-related stress (14%) is similarly higher than that of currently stressed women (5%).

At first blush, these findings are clearly counterintuitive and unexpected. Officers in our research group who were presented with the findings (see chapter 6) found them hard to accept, as did some social scientists with whom we shared the results. Explanations suggested to us for the data ranged from mean-spirited aspersions (sloppy methodology) to far-fetched assumptions about psychological sex difference (such as women are vastly more stress-resistant and resilient compared with men).

Table 4.1

Family-Related Stress Responses Reported by Male and Female Police Officers (rounded percentages)

Question	A great deal	Some	Very little	None
Q8a. Would you say that you are *currently* experiencing stress as a result of family-related problems? ($n = 201$)				
Men	14	29	30	27
Women	5	30	30	35
Q5. Do you feel that family-related stress has at some juncture affected your work motivation or performance? ($n = 207$)[a]				
Men	12	43	26	18
Women	7	27	39	27
Q6. Do you feel that work-related stress has ever affected your family life or home life? ($n = 208$)[b]				
Men	21	53	17	10
Women	5	56	26	14
Q7. Have you experienced difficulties balancing job and family responsibilities? ($n = 207$)[c]				
Men	14	38	28	20
Women	7	39	27	27

[a]Chi square, $df = 3$, $p = <.05$
[b]Chi square, $df = 3$, $p = <.07$
[c]Chi square, $df = 3$, $p = <.05$

Seniority, Age, and Family-Related Stress

A closer review of our response patterns provides the context for a different (and less abstruse) set of explanations. The point to keep in mind is that policing has until lately been a male-dominated occupation and that women have been recruited as police officers comparatively recently. This fact has

implications for the demographic composition of officer samples and populations and particularly for police age distri-
butions.

A disproportionate number of female officers had been employed by the department in the past 10 years. Three out of
four of the 45 women who responded (78%) indicated they had
10 years experience or less, compared to 29% of the 166 men.
The female officers were correspondingly younger than the
male officers. More than half (51%) the 37 women who responded were in the youngest (18–33 years) third of the age
distribution, compared to 28% of 125 men. The oldest age
group (39–58 years) encompassed 5% of the women and 36%
of the men. (More women, 14%, than men, 6%, refused to specify their age, but no inference may be drawn from this fact.)

There were also related differences in marital status. More
than two-thirds (68%) of the 166 men who responded reported that they are married, compared to 43% of the 45
women. A larger proportion of women were single (36%) or
divorced (18%), as compared with the men (14% and 8%,
respectively). Ten percent of the men and 4% of the women
did not reveal their marital status.

Table 4.2 displays stress-related responses by dichotomized
seniority groups. For each question, the suggestion is confirmed that family-related stress increases with seniority
level. The differences are especially marked with respect to
experienced "spillover." Fifty-eight percent of the older officers, as opposed to 35% of the younger officers, suggested
that family problems affect their work, and 78%—as opposed
to 54% of the less experienced officers—reported that occupational stress has affected their family life. More senior officers than young officers also said they have problems balancing work and family responsibilities, and more of the
older officers told us that they suffer family-related stress
than do younger, less experienced officers. Because middle-
aged, experienced officers are disproportionately male, this
difference may easily account for gender differences in reported family stress.

Questions worded like, "Do you feel that at some juncture
you were stressed?" may be affected by the time period available to experience stress. However, the older officers with

Table 4.2

Family-Related Stress Responses Reported by Officers of Varying Seniority Levels (rounded percentages)

Question	A great deal	Some	Very little	None
Q8a. Would you say that you are *currently* experiencing stress as a result of family-related problems? ($n = 223$)				
10 or fewer years	6	26	36	32
11 or more years	14	30	29	26
Q5. Do you feel that family-related stress has at some juncture affected your work motivation or performance? ($n = 230$)[a]				
10 or fewer years	7	28	34	31
11 or more years	11	47	24	17
Q6. Do you feel that work-related stress has ever affected your family life or home life? ($n = 232$)[b]				
10 or fewer years	12	42	28	17
11 or more years	22	56	14	7
Q7. Have you experienced difficulties balancing job and family responsibilities? ($n = 230$)[c]				
10 or fewer years	7	32	29	31
11 or more years	13	42	26	18

[a]Chi square, $df = 3$, $p = <.04$
[b]Chi square, $df = 3$, $p = <.001$
[c]Chi square, $df = 3$, $p = <.05$

more seniority also said they were currently encountering more family-related stress than were the less experienced, younger officers, although this difference was not sufficiently appreciable to reach statistical significance.[7]

---

[7]The response difference to this question did reach significance when we grouped respondents by age (18–38 vs. 39 years or older).

Reasons for Family-Related Stress

Table 4.3 lists occasions for current family-related stress as cited by the respondents. Time conflicts and marital crises head the list of difficulties.

Table 4.3

Reasons for Family-Related Stress

Reason	# of responses
Conflicts between working hours and family obligations; scheduling conflicts causing family complaints or problems	25
Other marital problems or marital conflicts; strained marriage	25
Childcare problems	16
Problems involving care of relatives; sick relatives	14
Problem relatives or members of household	14
Behavioral problems involving children; adolescents	12
Financial problems	12
Other	10

Typical schedule-related complaints include the following:

Job, home, family—just not enough time to take care of all of them.

Wife does not appreciate my taking overtime, says it takes quality time away from us.

Started working nights—spouse having problems adjusting.

Getting stuck on the day shift is not at all compatible with my home life.

Bizarre schedule affects my sleep, which makes me irritable.

Family will not respect my need for sleep.

Hours away from home, missing family functions, and holidays.

One officer wrote,

A close relative died—I wasn't eligible for bereavement. Family came across the country. I couldn't spend any time with them (I work evenings) because I've only been on the job two-plus years. I don't receive much time off.

Marriage-related comments as a rule were remarkably terse and sometimes poignant. Typical summary statements include the following:

Facing a divorce.

Disintegrating marriage.

Lack of communication.

Two divorces.

Relationship with girlfriend.

My wife hates me.

Although problem descriptions such as these were not age-specific, a number of other difficulties described by the respondents were situations that tend to arise in mature families—especially those with adolescent or young adult offspring:

Children not always doing what I know or think is right.

My son, a senior in high school, refuses to be committed to school.

Upcoming wedding of child.

Lost control of my two sons.

Grown-up kids remain in household with mother's permission.

Teenagers with their peer pressures and things they do to be accepted.

Wife's sons [ages] 23 and 19 not living with us—Bums, no jobs—Rather play Dungeons and Dragons and smoke than work—Wife pays their bills.

Twenty-eight-year-old son living at my home with girl-friend and baby.

Daughter's boyfriend relationship.

We are planning our daughter's wedding.

Children getting married and moving away.

Among family-related stressors encountered by the officers are marital problems that tend to arise over time. Other stressors consist of conflicts or crises that involve children who rebel, leave home or refuse to leave home, or manifest problems of their own. The stereotypic scenario of the newly married facing child care emergencies arises side by side with other—more frequent—problematic situations, which are apt to affect officers in their 30s, 40s, and 50s.

The age–stress relationship, however, also shows up in relation to other stressors, such as stress at work. In a matrix of Pearson's correlation coefficients (Table 4.4), the relationships between years of service and six assorted stress questions produced a negative coefficient in every case, with five of six relationships proving significant. One of the most impressive relationships we found with both seniority and gender involved responses to the first question in the survey, "Would you say that you are experiencing some work-related discomfort or stress?"

Other studies of occupational stress have also noted middle-age diminishments in morale. Joan Baker (1999) talked of a stage of "hitting the wall" in which officers become disillusioned and take a jaundiced view of their work. Ellen Kirschman, in her book *I Love a Cop* (1997), captured some of this disgruntlement and its sources. She described the wearying impact of occupational experiences combined with the cor-

Table 4.4

Correlations Among Age, Tenure, and Gender and Responses to Six Stress Questions

	Age	Tenure	Gender	Q1	Q31	Q32	Q33	Q34	Q62
Age	1.000								
Tenure	.709**	1.000							
Gender	-.221**	-.324**	1.000						
Q1	-.149*	-.234**	.234**	1.000					
Q31	-.216**	-.217**	.185*	.342**	1.000				
Q32	-.141*	-.236**	.156*	.505**	.608**	1.000			
Q33	-.121	-.186*	.092	.334**	.429**	.462**	1.000		
Q34	-.1	-.11	.105	.357**	.565**	.423**	.466**	1.000	
Q62	-.11	-.159	.140*	.656**	.319*	.491**	.302**	.383**	1.000

*p = <.05
**p = <.001
Q1 = Would you say that you are experiencing some work-related discomfort or stress?
Q31 = Do you feel that family-related stress has at some juncture affected your work motivation or performance?
Q32 = Do you feel that work-related stress has ever affected your family life or home life?
Q33 = Have you experienced difficulties balancing job and family responsibilities?
Q34 = Would you say that you are currently experiencing stress as a result of family-related problems?
Q62 = Would you say that you are currently experiencing stress as a result of work-related problems?

rosive effects of physical aging. The result is a perception of
the world in which

> politics, rather than fairness or justice, dominate the
> scene. The media are ten times more interested in the
> occasional police scandal than the thousands of everyday
> acts of courage and persistence. To make matters worse,
> your cop has likely discovered a few gray hairs, your
> children might be approaching adolescence, and your
> parents are showing signs of old age. (p. 42)

For some officers, the intersection between diminished career aspirations and limited opportunities and organizational
supports undergirds a fondly advertised cynical view of law
enforcement, as a career and as an occupation. As Kirschman
(1997) described this perspective,

> Now they feel locked into policing but locked out of the
> rewards that policing once offered. The career that prom-
> ised them twenty to twenty-five years of fulfillment
> seems over in ten.
>
> During this period, all past decisions may come into
> question. Why did he or she choose this career, marry
> young, fail to finish college, work so hard for a master's
> degree, have kids, not have kids? How competent is he
> or she really; where did all the money go; where did all
> the time go; is he or she a good parent, a good spouse,
> a good cop?
>
> This is suffering. Officers may doubt that anyone un-
> derstands or cares about their welfare and what they
> have to deal with on the street. They become fixated on
> personal concerns, especially salary, schedules, and other
> compensation issues. Appreciation of their work is so
> hard to come by that some cops will begin to file for
> fifteen minutes of overtime in a job that years ago they
> might have performed for free.
>
> Those who are deeply disillusioned may become in-
> creasingly irritated and critical of the organization they
> once naively regarded as a benevolent parent. They see
> their jobs as the most important, yet least acknowledged.

They have only criticism for supervisors and administrators who do nothing right and never know what is going on.... Their world has been reduced to "us" and "them," and *they* are worthy only of contempt. People are "perps" and "slime bags." Successful cops are "brown nosers" and "fast trackers." Racism, sexism, and all the other "isms" that support an egocentric world view are rampant. (p. 44)

Fortunately, publicly promulgated cynicism can be expressive behavior, somewhat on the order of psychological fireworks. Such statements are not summaries of a person's privately held beliefs or attitudes. They are designed, rather, to draw attention to the person's feelings. Early police psychology literature assiduously discussed cynicism among officers as a personality trait and may have missed the point. The point—at least, among middle-aged officers—has mostly to do with unrealized hope, unachieved aspiration, unrequited dedication, and unrewarded loyalty. The message is one of growing hopelessness, disappointment, and bitterness. The issue is age-related (and career-related) and has to do with occupational stress.

Family problems can be exacerbated by occupational stress because stress has a way of "spilling over." Even when an officer makes a point of becoming psychologically compartmentalized and of leaving work problems at work, this prized gambit is less protective and more transparent than the average officer may imagine. Studies of police families have found that some officers' wives complain that their husbands are uncommunicative and tend to converse with their partners while remaining strangers at home. If an officer walks about with clenched teeth, he or she is apt to be perceived as engaging in noncompanionable behavior.

Alienated officers are likely to extend or apply their jaundiced perspective to family problems and to take such problems less lightly than they would if they were not already perpetually aggravated. Frustrations at home may similarly affect the officers' work, especially because they are apt to keep family problems to themselves.

To the extent to which this process of stress amplification is operative among male officers, female officers may be less susceptible to it. Gender differences in work-related attitudes are known to be negligible, but norms about family relationships are not. Female officers may be less reluctant to share work-related problems than male officers and therefore might experience less stress, even when they and their families age. Given this possibility, it is hard to predict what gender differences we may find as women in policing acquire more seniority and reach more stress-prone age levels. But our study suggests that older female officers will probably experience increments in stress. Our gender differences tended to dissipate when we compared young (younger than age 34) male and female officers.[8] But half the differences also dissipated between less young (older than age 33) cohorts of men and women. We were led to conclude that gender differences in reported stress can come about because young female officers are less stressed are than tenured male officers.[9]

---

[8]For three of six questions, there were no differences in responses of young male and female officers. The remaining differences were too small to reach statistical significance. With officers who had been on the job 10 or fewer years, only one significant finding emerged. In answer to the question, "Do you feel that family-related stress has at some juncture affected your work motivation or performance?" the proportion of the men who responded "often" or "sometimes" totaled 42%, compared with 12% of the women.

[9]Multivariate analyses confirmed the conclusion that seniority is related to stress level. We completed two types of multivariate analysis: ordinary least squares regression and a probit analysis. Both used a stress index scale comprising responses to three questions as the dependent variable. Both models had a significant F value, showing that the model as a whole predicts variation in the stress scale, but neither model explained more than 5% of the variance (Adj. R^2 + 0.0483). More to the point, "years of service" was the only independent variable in either model that achieved statistical significance.

5

Perceptions of Conflict and Discrimination

A s our interviews and focus groups have shown, the members of our urban police department appear individually committed to contributing to the public good. Doing things for people—especially, those who are disadvantaged—is a source of satisfaction and pride seemingly to all the officers in the department. But convergence around such goals does not readily translate into harmony and acceptance within the department.

The tradition of the city in which the department is located has prominently included patronage and other vestiges of machine politics, as well as organized responses to this tradition. The reaction against patronage practices in the police has included rancorous labor disputes and a series of labor contracts that place a premium on seniority as a criterion for assignments and promotion. Residual practices that could be interpreted as leaving room for patronage (such as management involvement in the promotion of patrol officers to detectives) are strongly resented, a fact reflected in the survey results (see chapter 3).

Feelings about race and gender relations have evolved against the background of strongly felt concerns about the fairness of promotion and assignment decisions. They have also developed against the background of rapid change in the composition of the police force over a short period of time. The change has intersected with the issue of fairness, in that both traditional and nontraditional officers have scrutinized their careers in terms of the equity of available opportunities. Accelerated change has also raised questions about how fully such change has been accepted. Some of the older or White male officers can be less hospitable than others to their newly hired colleagues, and the latter may have legitimate concerns about how well they have been accepted. Doubts and resentments can produce tensions between groups. These in turn can become a nagging problem that acquires a life of its own and is a continuing source of stress.

One of our early interviewees—a Black female officer—delineated the nature of this problem as she saw it. Her view of the department was generally extremely positive. She prized her own assignment [as a Drug Abuse Resistance Education (DARE) officer], and felt she had "been blessed" with opportunities for personal development. But the officer recalled her first patrol assignment as an unhappy period in her life. She was then the solitary minority officer in her precinct, and she had felt rejected, excluded, and "lonely." She indicated that she was saved by the appearance of a second ethnic minority (male Hispanic) officer. Later, she felt reinforced by a "network" of fellow Black officers who supported each other. She adjudged such "bonding" among members of racial groups as inevitable at the time, but she also worried about the continued existence and obduracy of groups and cliques in the department. In building bridges between groups, she felt, it was too easy to revert to expressions of "us" and "them" and to resume self-segregating attitudes and behavior.

The promotional fairness issue arose for this officer because she had been seconded to the detective division but had ultimately not been retained there. It was important—she felt—to not react to such experiences by remaining bitter and antagonistic, thereby escalating conflict and rejection.

As it happens, the experiences and observations of this officer go to the crux of the complex issues of stress, coping, and race in police departments. For one, Black officers in police stress studies generally highlight the benefits of intraracial bonding. Haarr and Morash (1999) thus reported that their study participants prominently mentioned "forming bonds with coworkers with whom one shares a racial bond." They speculated that

> African American officers . . . might feel that their only recourse in responding to [workplace] stress is to form bonds with coworkers of the same race. Moreover, African American officers may be more aware of turning to members of their own racial group. Caucasian officers, in contrast, despite their tendency to turn to other Caucasian officers, do not label that tendency as "forming bonds with somebody with whom one shares a racial bond," although that might be the case (p. 325).

Mutual support can be a constructive and positive coping strategy—especially for people who are newly arrived at a setting or an occupation and have questions about the wholeheartedness of their acceptance. In that sense, bonding is not only an understandable reaction but also, arguably, a healthy one. The problem is that of potentially diminishing returns when the strategy has become functionally autonomous of its origin and has resulted in continued self-segregation, which reinforces social distance. The question arises about the solidity of a blue line that is sharply compartmentalized. Moreover, the corollary of social support can be hostility to out-group members and the perpetuation of conflict between in-groups and out-groups.

Results From the Surveys

In rankings of stress, there were variations in responses to race-related questions. Discrimination ranked low among perceived sources of stress, but racial relations in the department were judged stressful by more than half the respondents and by two-thirds of the Black respondents. One of four (28%) Black officers indicated that racial tension in the department was very stressful to them (see Table 5.1). Current race relations were of somewhat greater concern than past race relations, implying a lack of progress in this area.

Table 5.2 delineates responses to a question that invited descriptions of race relations in the department. The most prevalent view was that the problems in the area were not excessively serious. As one officer put it,

> Relations are good. There are those on both sides who at times can make things difficult. However, most people realize who they are and what they're about, and they disregard it and go on being good working officers.

Another officer wrote,

> Not perfect but fairly good. The department is in fact integrated, in that the officers voluntarily choose to work together. A comparison to the fire department which has minority employees but is completely segregated is valuable.

Other responses in the same vein about race relations in the department include the following:

Table 5.1

Stress Attributed by Black and White Officers to Racial Tension in the Department (percentages)

	Black officers (N = 39)	White officers (N = 163)
Very stressful	28.2	14.1
Stressful	41.0	34.9
Not stressful	17.9	42.9
No response	12.8	7.9

Table 5.2

Respondents' Characterization of Racial Relations in the Department

Characterization	# of responses
No problem; nothing serious; fair	69
Problem involving preferential treatment of minority officers	42
Mutual mistrust; suspicion; resentment	29
Crisis; extremely bad relations	19
Problem that of militant minority	19
Male White prejudice and discrimination	18
Department is racially segregated, divided	17
No problem where I am located	16
The problem is not surfaced and discussed	13
There is a problem (unspecified)	11
There may be a problem somewhere in the department	10
Other	9

The response frequencies in this table cannot be interpreted as reflecting the numerical distribution of race-related attitudes in the department. For one, ethnic minority officers are underrepresented in our sample; second, respondents to this question are self-selected, and their views may differ from those of the nonrespondents.

Livable contemporary.

It mirrors the state in society generally.

Better than on the street.

I feel that the problems I witness are the same every-where.

My experience—we all work well together.

I think for the most part, the department is a pretty close-knit group.

Not as terrible as people think they are.

Gradually improving.

Adequate.

On the opposite extreme, some respondents felt that the race relations problem had reached crisis proportions. One officer explained, "There currently are two police departments—one Black and one White. There is no unity, except in very few circumstances." Other comments include,

Sucks.

It is getting worse.

Very tense.

Racial tension is high and has been for some time.

As bad or worse than race relations on the street.

Blacks usually side with Blacks. Whites with Whites.

The Roshamon Phenomenon[1]

Officers who thought there was a problem in the department differed in the way they explained the nature of the problem that they perceived. Although some respondents characterized the situation as one of mutual mistrust, others were less evenhanded in their assessment.

Two diametrically opposite, nonoverlapping views of the situation emerged in the responses. One perspective blamed the tension on the ethnic minority officers or alleged that the officers were preferentially treated, thereby occasioning resentment:

African Americans seem to complain about everything and anything.

Blacks seem to be making mountains out of molehills.

---

[1]"Roshamon" is the title of a Japanese film concerned with the psychology of perception. Several protagonists in an incident relate their independent versions of what transpired. The accounts describe discrepant and incompatible events, leaving viewers with the inference that the "truth" is not ascertainable.

There is a growing number of officers who cry racism to cover their mistakes or shortcomings.

Minorities are not held nearly as accountable for their actions [as] Whites are.

Double standard with enforcement of departmental rules —Blacks, lightly enforced; Whites, heavily enforced.

The department takes minorities' concerns too seriously when making decisions.

The current mayor and commissioner are politically correct and not fair.

The opposite view of the problem attributed it to the prejudice of a White in-group and to persistent discriminatory practices favoring White people or White males:

Many [Black] officers are treated differently than White (majority) officers, but they are afraid to come forward in fear of retaliation.

Blacks do not have political people that they can turn to.

Black officers do not receive the same treatment or representation from the department or the union.

Racism is primarily done in the dark behind closed doors.

Officers' attitudes are racist and prejudiced.

Personally I feel that the department not only needs to address racial relations—they need to look into sexism. I find by being a minority and not of the dominant sex I'm being convicted of a crime without having a trial.

The perception of continuing discrimination is reflected in the way Black officers perceive their own career opportunities (Tables 5.3 and 5.4). Three of four Black officers said that their own opportunities had been constrained by discrimination; most of these officers felt that their opportunities had been constrained a great deal. Most Black officers also said they had been subjected to discrimination at work. The con-

Table 5.3

Responses to the Question, "Do you feel that you personally have experienced racial or gender discrimination at work?" (*percentages*)

	Often	Sometimes	Very occasionally	Never
Gender				
Male officers (N = 166)	7.3	33.8	19.2	39.7
Female officers (N = 45)	16.3	37.2	27.9	18.6
Race				
Black officers (N = 39)	24.2	45.5	9.1	21.2
White non-Hispanic officers (N = 163)	6.5	32.7	21.6	39.2
Other[a] (N = 18)	18.8	31.3	25.0	25.0

Chi-square, $p < .001$.
[a]"Other" largely comprises Hispanic officers. The responses of this group fall midway between those of Black and White officers. However, fairly small numbers (single-digit cells in each table) make the difference potentially unreliable.

trasting perspective is also in evidence: 4 of 10 White officers contended that racial considerations had been an obstacle to their opportunities for advancement.

The contrast and inconsistency are striking, but comparable mirror-image charges alleging favoritism in the dispensation of rewards recur in other settings. *The New York Times* dramatically illustrated this fact in a series of in-depth reports covering institutions ranging from metropolitan newspapers to military training camps. A capstone article characterized the situation as a "stubbornly enduring racial divide" encompassing "remoteness and distrust in places of work, learning and worship" (Sack & Elder, 2000, p. A1). The article also pointed out that in public opinion polls "whites expressed a certain fatigue with racial issues" and "were three times as likely as blacks—33 percent to 10 percent—to say that too

Table 5.4

Perceived Impact of Discrimination on One's Opportunities for Advancement (percentages)

	Often	Sometimes	Very occasionally	Never
Race				
Black officers (N = 39)	39.5	31.6	18.4	10.5
White non-Hispanic officers (N = 163)	10.1	33.0	23.4	33.5
Hispanic and other (N = 49)	17.6	35.3	5.9	41.2
Gender				
Male officers (N = 166)	7.2	28.9	24.0	38.0
Female officers (N = 45)	22.2	37.8	16.0	22.0

Chi-square, $p < .001$.

much has been made in recent years of the problems facing black people" (p. A23). A survey recently conducted by the Police Foundation (Weisburd, Greenspan, Hamilton, and Williams, 2000) explored another aspect of the racial divide in policing. The authors asserted that the disconnection is of such magnitude that "even the apparently strong culture of policing does not transcend it" (p. 8). They reported that their officer respondents differed markedly in their views about the fairness and equity of police practices. Whereas most White officers, for example, disagreed with the contention that "police officers often treat Whites better than Blacks and other minorities," more than half the Black officers concurred with this assessment. The majority of Black officers also endorsed the view that police are likely to use physical force against poor and minority citizens, an assertion denied by 9 of 10 White officers. And whereas two-thirds of Black officers felt that community policing could decrease use-of-force incidents, most of the White officers disagreed. (Male officers and female officers did not differ in their responses to the survey questions.)

Gender Relations

Tables 5.3 and 5.4 also present the responses of male and female officers to questions relating to gender discrimination. Whereas more than half the female officers said they had been discriminated against, an even larger proportion (nearly two-thirds) of the women contended that their advancement opportunities were limited on account of their gender.

A confirmation of gender bias is provided by Figure 5.1, which details the responses to the question, "Do you feel more comfortable or less comfortable when you work with someone of the opposite sex?" Only a small number of women responded "less comfortable" (although a few said "more comfortable"), but an appreciable proportion of male officers (45%) said they were less comfortable having to work with a female officer. Older male officers were more likely to prefer working with another male officer (46%) than those of less seniority (40%). The survey concurrently shows no reluctance among any respondents to work with an officer of a different race. To the extent to which ethnic prejudice may exist in the department, it does not extend to lack of trust or

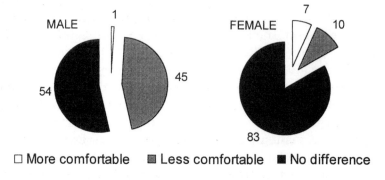

☐ More comfortable   ▨ Less comfortable   ■ No difference

Figure 5.1. Responses to the question "Do you feel more or less comfortable when you work with someone of the opposite sex?" by gender (rounded percentages)

Table 5.5

Attitudes Relating to Interventions That Address the Issues of Race and Gender in the Question, "Do you feel that enough attention has been given to the issues of race and gender in the department?" (percentages)

	Black officers (N = 39)	White officers (N = 163)	Hispanic and other officers (N = 18)
Not enough attention	82	19	50
Enough attention	8	42	39
Too much attention	0	23	11
No response	10	16	0

confidence at work. By contrast, feelings about female officers appear to be related to traditional pugilistic conceptions of police work.

Some Solutions

The police department had been concerned for some time about race (and gender) relations and had made efforts to address the problem through inservice training. In addition to highlighting the subject in conventional curricula, specialized workshops have been made available to members of the department.

One such exercise—an interracial "circle"—was experienced by the DARE officer we referred to above, who characterized it as an example of what was needed. She felt, however, that too much venting, reciprocal recrimination, and mutual stereotyping are unconstructive. She also wondered how much transfer one would expect to relations at work and whether the benefit would be confined to those who least needed the experience.

Table 5.5 lists survey responses relating to departmental activities in this area. The overwhelming majority of Black officers felt that more such interventions were needed. However, the dominant response among White officers was that too much attention had been paid to interracial issues.

The difference in responses provides documentation for the thesis that dominant group perspectives about race and gender relations in the department—and no doubt in other departments—are sharply at variance. Planned change is essential, and it must be undertaken with vigor. However, client involvement in such change is more important than usual, because any efforts that are seen as favoring one race or gender group would undergird the resentments of the other. This paradigm is a classic example of "high-gradient" or "incongruent" change (Lewin, 1947), which can be achieved only by surfacing and working through predictable resistances.

6

Data Feedback Sessions

A ction research presupposes a division of labor that rele-
gates some clerical tasks to consultants, whose academic
training qualifies them to code and enter numerical data and
to prepare legible (and, one hopes, comprehensible) tables of
the sort that appear in the previous pages.

The tasks of digesting the data and of considering it as a
basis for action fall to the client organization, which is the
"consumer" of the research that it has instigated. In our
study, a group of police officers (our planning groups) had
originated a set of questions that had yielded findings. The
consultants (ourselves) had tabulated these findings. The
next stage involved the sharing of data in feedback sessions.

Full-day workshops were scheduled, one for the project
participants and another for the suburban department. Pack-
ages of graphs and tables were distributed in advance of
these workshops, and the officers were invited to analyze the
data and draw inferences from them. We hoped these inferences would culminate in useful recommendations for action.
(The process is incestuous, in that proposals that emerge are
presumed to be data-based, and data are assumed to inspire
ideas for change.)

To facilitate discussions, we subdivided the survey data
into subject areas. For the first workshop, these areas were

(a) problems related to politics and administration, (b) problems related to racial and gender relations in the department, and (c) work- and family-related stress and stress management. Each subject area was to be dealt with in a separate session, with discussion informed by presumptively relevant statistics. A dinner—which included the spouses of the officers—was to climax the proceedings.

The material for the sessions was accompanied by a cover letter, which read

MESSAGE TO FELLOW MEMBERS
OF THE GROUP

Enclosed you will find a summary of responses to our Survey. Please review this information in advance of the meeting.

We are also supplying you with three sets of data relating to the three sessions we have scheduled. You'll see that we have tried to present these data in a way that should make it painless to read and digest them.

You will also receive an assignment that involves your participation in one of the sessions. If you have been asked to help outline a problem, you can prepare your informal presentation in advance. Please be sure to use the survey results, though you can go beyond them, if need be, in outlining the problem as you see it. If you have been assigned to discuss suggestions for possible courses of action, you must draw on the discussion that precedes your presentation. But there really is nothing to prevent you from thinking about possible suggested interventions in advance of the meeting. Please be sure to consider practicality of implementation in thinking about proposals.

We attached a prefatory note to each set of data. In relation to the first session in the city department, our concern was with not downplaying the intensity of respondents' feelings, while sparing the commissioner the prospect of an unproductive gripe session. We wrote

The enclosed tables and graphs suggest that the subject

we call *"Politics and Administration"* heads the list of identified sources of stress.

In considering these data you will have to focus on practices and activities that result in perceptions of unfairness
that produce resentments. You might also recall, however, that perceptions of a problem can reduce or mag-
nify its seriousness. Perceptions and feelings (such as fear
of crime, for example) are a problem in their own right.
Sometimes interventions that reduce misperceptions or
deal with feelings can help solve a problem.

The second session, on racial and gender relations, carried
a different risk, which was that of recriminations and accusations based on divergent perceptions of race relations in
the city department. Our note read

> The enclosed tables and graphs suggest that there are
> differences in the way this problem is perceived by dif-
> ferent members of the Department.
>
> One of the issues that invites consideration is that
> some of the differences are based on perceptions that are
> almost diametrically opposed to each other. On the other
> hand, the data also suggest that the problem has not
> reached crisis proportions, and may therefore be ame-
> nable to timely interventions.

For the third session, on work- and family-related stress,
we wanted to draw attention to unexpected findings and
hoped that the group might consider the differences that
were highlighted by the survey results:

> One of the more surprising results of the Survey is the
> finding that our female respondents report less family-
> related stress than our male respondents.
>
> Further exploration of this finding suggests that it has
> to do with date of appointment, which in turn produces
> differences in age. Young officers are frequently unmar-
> ried or recently married. Family-related stress shows up
> as families mature and children grow older. This tells us

something about how to target assistance to officers under stress.

The risks we had envisaged in fact would never have materialized. The city commissioner's charismatic presence and his participation were warmly appreciated by the group of officers. Moreover, the session was one of the commissioner's last acts in office.

The commissioner's surprise resignation had diminished the incentive for the group to advance a list of recommendations for his consideration. Partly as a result, the sessions were less task-oriented than were the deliberations of the suburban police department, whose long-term chief (who attended most of the suburban session) was continuing in office.

Results From the Workshop Session

In relation to each survey topic, the data were reviewed by one of the officers and commented on by others. Consultants acted as summarizers at the conclusion of each discussion.

With regard to the first topic, the summarizer said the group had noted the intensity of feelings. He pointed out that politics-related feelings were probably stronger in the department than in most other municipalities because of past events that had left a residue of bitterness. The summarizer said that "getting beyond [the feelings] is probably one of the challenges."

The group discussed supervisors (a topic that had not emerged in the survey) and pressures external to the police department. The group talked of "responsible" and "credible" community groups with whom relationships could be established. Another suggestion related to incentive pay for officers who acquired special skills useful to the department. Also suggested was an assessment center for promotional candidates, and it was concluded that one antidote to adverse media coverage could be proactivity in disseminating information.

A lighter moment occurred when an officer raised the subject of "qualifications for the commissioner." This topic was tactfully transmuted. It was concluded that officers should "have enough information to understand the direction the department wants to go in and where they could help the department move in that direction."

One highlight of the second session, on racial and gender relations, was an appeal by the president of the African American group for solidarity in the department's ranks. The session summarizer reported that

> ... We heard about or talked about the possibility of creating a new code of ethics, looking at ways to keep more unity among officers, more of a sense of pride and job in the department, a sense that all of the officers are on the same side ... and several [in the group] talked about building standards or discipline or ways of having a situation in which officers felt pride and felt unity, and the difficulties of doing that.

Participants speculated that generational differences in stress levels could be exacerbated by diversity among the younger officers and that "for Black females, there is a kind of double whammy." In relation to racial segregation, someone mentioned that "women may be segregating themselves in terms of choosing female partners." And some male officers wondered whether older women approaching retirement might require special (unspecified) assistance.

The group agreed that the departmental problem of race relations was a serious and recalcitrant one. The fact that some respondents "think that too much attention is paid to the problem" suggested that interventions could meet with resistance. As for the deployment of cultural awareness training, "the perception (was that it) may not have been as effective as possible." The officers thought that if such training were to be done, it would be best done by officers. They also suggested that "perhaps officers should be rotated through internal affairs to understand what the standards are and how they are applied."

In the third session, on work- and family-related stress, the group took note of discrepancies in the data about the extent of problem sharing with spouses. The officers decided that differences in the extent of sharing reported might be related to differences in definitions of problems to be shared.

Gender differences in family-related stress were described as "shocking" to the group. Some officers proposed that women might be more resilient than men, that they "didn't allow things to bother them as much" or "don't show as much stress." The officers then concluded, after discussion, that in time, women "would be heading for the same problems that their older male partners are currently facing."

With regard to stress amelioration, it was suggested that "an early warning system might be established to help officers to proactively head off problems." This suggestion, however, was at once rejected on the grounds that "any official system that was developed would probably not be trusted by the rank and file."

A number of suggestions for extensions of Employee Assistance Program (EAP) activity were advanced by a captain who had supervised the program, and he felt it especially important to expand the involvement of EAP with police family members. The captain also suggested "that life transition training or (counseling related to) reintegration back into civilian life could be helpful, as members of this department become older."

A final issue addressed by the group was that of opportunities for officer job enrichment or personal development. It was suggested that the department could "allow police officers to develop their own specialty areas within the rank of police officer."

Results From the Suburban Department Feedback Session

The workshop in the suburban police department was relatively unstructured, in that data had been distributed but no topics had been assigned. However, the discussion was tape recorded, preserving the flavor as well as the content of the deliberations. Some of the opening banter is illustrative of the flavor:

> Project member: And we lied about our drinking
> Group member: Yeah, we did notice that.
> Project member: And they pointed that out to us. They says, ah,—Are you all teetotalers up there?—75% of you said you don't drink. And I says, no, you don't understand, you got to specify what drinking is. Do you say, do you go home and have 4 or 5 beers after work, and I will say, Yeah, but that is not drinking. When I get up to 12 or 13, yeah, now I am drinking. There is a big difference.

The officers indicated as an alternative hypothesis that drinking levels might be related to stress levels. In comparing sources of police stress in the city and the suburb, one officer asserted that, "If anybody said that the intensity of our job [in the suburb] is the same as theirs [in the city], they'd be fooling themselves."

On a more serious note, the group of officers concluded that age-related stress differences made sense to them, because "our families are getting older, and our parents are getting older, and we have to take care of them, so we are getting crushed on both ends." On the other hand, the group felt that some of the younger officers might have serious problems. One officer recalled that "when I worked traffic, it was a real hassle balancing job and family because my wife would work during the days, and I would be stuck dragging the kids into court with me, and stuff like that." Another officer said, "I think the ['never' answers] all account to the ones that don't have kids."

External Diplomacy

There was consensus that the inflexibility of the courts in scheduling police officers' testimony exacerbated family problems. One officer argued that "as far as external forces

[go], it seems to me that the courts and the way they mess up your family life is the biggest issue we face." The courts were said to respect the preferences of attorneys and to be indifferent to the needs of officers: "Their whole attitude is, 'Well, you're getting paid.'" But no line was seen to exist between indifference to officers and contempt for the police: "We all agreed that the court has listed us lower than the plankton at the bottom of the ocean." As one manifestation of contempt, the town court was said to disregard the working schedules and family obligations of the officers:

> They don't even have one bit of concern of police scheduling and shifts that we are on 24 hours a day. They cater more to the attorney who needs to close on a house somewhere in Lancaster, before they care about who has kids, and what day, or what part of the shift, what tour they are on, if they get off at 7:00 or if they had a late arrest—they don't care.

Indifference to officers, who work on a 24-hour day and may have family emergencies, was illustrated with examples.

> I was out of town and even gave them notice—I gave them written notice—and they scheduled me for a trial on the day before I had to come back, and they wouldn't adjourn it for me. . . . I came back early, came back that day, and when I came back they adjourned it for the attorney.

* * *

> After we have changed plans, gone into court, "Oh, half an hour ago my attorney requested an adjournment and we gave it to him." "Excuse me, I just came back in from out of town for court, and now you're telling me that my request for adjournment—whatever the reason was— they don't even care if it was a family member needing an operation—we just told you to be here, you gotta be here."

The officers in the group decided that the department's

chief—who had not yet arrived at the session—should be asked to continue to address the problem through high-level diplomacy, as "one department head to another." If the response to such overtures was that "[the courts are still] going out of their way to mess with our people," the officers felt that the chief should use a more confrontational approach. As an example of available forceful courses of action, some more or less drastic initiatives were proposed:

> . . . and the bottom line in all of this is that we need to send a message to these people that you want to make our lives miserable, we can make your lives miserable . . . you want to jerk my guys around, I will schedule every goddamn arraignment for a Friday and you can sit there Monday, Tuesday, Wednesday, and Thursday arraigning no one . . . and you will sit here until 10 o'clock at night, if you want to jerk our guys around . . . and, also, the day shift sergeant controls the prisoner movement down to the court . . . well, my personal feeling is, I'll keep that goddamn cell door shut all day long, and they'll get them when I say they get them, not when the judge calls for them. Okay, and we'll screw up their court and we'll screw up their scheduling or they are going to sit down and work with us . . . and if this is the way we are going to operate, that is the way we are going to operate, because we are not taking this anymore. You are not going to tie up our road patrol needlessly, you are not going to keep our officers here because you think they are making too much money, this is the way it is going to be. You want to jerk us around, we have ways of jerking you around too, and I think that is the approach we have to take.

There was concern about the perceived hostility of judges to the police. "How many times," asked one officer, "have you heard judges from the bench blast the chief and blast the department in a public forum?"

One officer produced his calculation of the department's arrest productivity, which he felt deserved the gratitude— rather than the antagonism—of the courts:

> I did the math, if you average it out . . . [the city's] officer
> makes 19 arrests per year, our guys are making almost
> 27. I mean, the chief made a comment the other day,
> pound for pound, there is no police department out there
> that does more than we do, and I think somebody has
> got to step up and point these facts out, that our guys
> are busting their butts, and our guys are doing a hell of
> a lot of work with the resources that we have and should
> not be getting jerked around by a couple of two-bit town
> justices. . . . They should be applauding us every day
> when they get on the bench, and say, "Okay, folks, by
> the way, the police department is the finest around—I
> am glad to be here adjudicating the fine work they do."
> No, they stand up and start bashing us in court.

The officers argued that because courts are consumers of
police products, they should appreciate police productivity.
As one officer put it, "They are riding on our shirttails, and
if we did not effectively do our job, as actively as we be
doing, they have nothing—what they have is a couple of civil
cases, that is all they will have."

Tension in the criminal justice system, the officers suggested, has to be reduced because the alternative is dysfunctional, as well as stress producing.

Internal Diplomacy

The suburban officers were genuinely impressed by the extent to which they had attributed distress to problems in their
organization. They went to some length, however, to insist
that they were not surprised by this fact:

> I've been here 12 years now and I have been involved in
> the union for 10, and I've always heard time and time
> again that job stresses have very little to do with the
> actual functioning of the job—as far as the handling of
> calls and things like that—but the stress is from internal
> pressure that comes from the department, and after look-
> ing at these charts and looking at the way everything
> was answered, that came out exactly the way I expected

it would: That the biggest threats on police officers is not the job on the road, it is how the job is being done internally as far as the directions the department is going, the leadership, the promotion—that seems to be what drives people the most and what upsets them the most . . . we seem to handle that [street] stuff well, it is the internal stuff that bothers us the most, and that comes through loud and clear.

What the officers said surprised them were the differences in the city and suburban department responses. An officer noted,

One thing that jumped out at me, and that did surprise me, was our feelings were more intense than [those in the city]. . . . I would have thought that . . . they would have had more negative feelings toward their administration than we would, but that didn't come through.

The officer hypothesized that "maybe it works that way because more people know our administrators and our chief, because they came up through the ranks, so you had a lot more time to build up animosity to people."

The officer said that one reason for being surprised is that an ethnically homogenous department such as the suburban one could be expected to be more harmonious:

I never thought that we would have more negative feelings toward our administration than [the city] had toward theirs. Especially when you take into account racial diversity, gender diversity, things of that nature—let's face it, we are all White males, with the exception of three people.
[Female:] Four.
Four now, four now, okay. But I did not think that it would come out that way. . . . The same thing came through with supervision. We had more negative feelings toward our direct supervision than they did. . . . I am really surprised at this because you have Blacks supervising Whites, Whites supervising Blacks, more females su-

pervising males, more females supervising. I would have thought for sure that you [city] guys would have had more negative feelings than we would. We basically have White males supervising other White males. . . . So we don't have all those built-in barriers that their system has, yet we don't seem to get along as good.

In making such assessments, the group of officers took proportions and differences seriously, analyzing them as meticulously as any overconscientious trained social scientist. For example,

Number 18 on page 4, only 35% said very stressful. . . . Yeah, page 2 if you look at number 7 it is better than it used to be, somebody must be doing something right, probably shortly after I became sergeant.

* * *

These two political influences, internal and external, they are just absolutely the opposite. . . . You are talking about 15% saying not stressful and the rest would be either stressful or very stressful. . . .

From what I understand, years ago you had to pay off a councilman to get your job. I think years ago, the people would have said the external politics had more to do with how the department was being ruined, and certainly people don't feel that way anymore.

One area of concern to the suburban officers was the quality of their supervision. They did not complain about being oversupervised or about being unfairly dealt with. Instead, they felt they were undersupervised. The officers said, for example, that their evaluations were not informative to them. As one officer put it, "What do they mean, evaluate? . . . Our personal evaluations don't point out any flaws, they don't point out anything." One reason for their nonevaluative evaluations that the officers cited was that supervisors had too little contact with them at work:

I've heard a million times that the supervisor isn't seeing

my work, and I'm getting evaluated by a supervisor who hasn't been on a call with me in 7 or 8 years. . . . When you turn your arrests in at the end of the day, who the hell even knows if they are doing it right? . . . If it's right, it's right, if it is wrong, it's wrong, who the hell knows? But the supervisor doesn't know. The supervisor doesn't know what you are doing.

Some supervisors were described as taking a hands-on interest and covering or responding to calls, but others were judged noteworthy for their habitual absence:

They don't even know what's happening. A car chase, a guy with a gun, and they get on the radio and they ask, is there something going on that I should know about? There is all of these police cars flying down the road . . .

The concern was, in part, a concern with quality control, with fellow officers who might not be carrying their load but who were not being monitored to verify that they were doing their jobs.

You got the guys that work, and then you got the guys that don't. Why isn't the supervisor out there telling these guys to do something? [They] come in here and sign in, and then sign out when [they] go home—[they] don't do anything.

The officers felt that a supervisor should not be routinely underfoot, but malfeasance or misfeasance had to be corrected because "if somebody is doing something wrong, that will make [all of] us all look bad." It was noted that unions are often charged with defending those who do a poor job, but the union president said his group favored retraining any police officer who became involved in difficulties or did not earn his keep.

I said, we are more responsible for the 90 guys doing it right, than we are for the 1 or 2 guys doing it wrong.

The 1 or 2 guys doing it wrong are endangering the other 90. . . . If some guy is an idiot and can't do his job right and you gotta go out there, and he is your only cover, and the department wants to bring this guy in and re-train him, they think the union is going to stand in the way? Retrain his ass, I don't give a shit. . . . I had super-visors go, yeah, right, but then you will be in here jump-ing up and down! You're wrong. If this guy's unsafe and this guy don't know his job—and we know a few guys we're talking about—and you wonder how the fuck does this guy get through the day, and if you want to bring this guy in and show him how to do the job right, we'll accommodate you.

The dispatchers. Dispatchers are the key sources of infor-mation for officers, and they inevitably become targets of dis-gruntlement. Most officers, in general, feel they get frequent misinformation or not enough information to do their work. They also tend to feel that they often get misdirected or badly advised and that their dispatchers follow dysfunctional, in-flexible bureaucratic rituals. Dispatchers, being civilians, are deemed to be poorly informed about street-level police re-alities.

On the other hand, officers do not generally feel that uni-formed personnel should do dispatching, as they usually did in the past. For one, dispatching is not a prized assignment:

When we did it, there were a lot of guys in there that didn't want to be there. . . . I don't think it is an issue of throwing [the civilians] out, I think it is an issue that they should be trained better, and they should be held ac-countable a hell of a lot more.

Given that civilian dispatchers are obviously here to stay, the suburban officers had to consider constructive alterna-tives having to do with training, supervision, and cross-fertilization between officers and dispatchers—with the pro-viso that "it is the patrolman who should have the most input on how things should be done."

Supervision of dispatchers (a problem deemed to be related to the issue of supervision, generally) was said to call for the cross-checking of responses of the dispatchers by proactive police supervisors:

> If a lieutenant hears something go out over a radio that doesn't sound right, they should be in there, and they should have the power to do something about it. I don't think he needs somebody standing over them because that will never happen, but if a lieutenant sits there and hears you ask for information, and the lieutenant knows that the dispatcher hung up on a call that was an in-progress call, and he knows that dispatcher hung up, [then] after that call is complete, that lieutenant should be in dispatch to find out what the hell happened, listen to the tapes and say you screwed up, and you put that officer's life in danger, that is a mistake that will not happen again, and I am putting you on notice right now. That is not going to be tolerated. But the lieutenant doesn't have that power, and I don't think that half the lieutenants want it either, because that would mean that they would actually have to do something.

Supervision was also said to imply coordination of activities to ensure that the dispatchers' time was deployed to the best advantage:

> When it gets busy, there are two or three other guys back there that are dispatchers and they don't help each other. They shouldn't make [one] person work the radio, run the license plate, and make the phone call [if] a car on the road asks them to call somebody, while the other two or three people are reading magazines.

A third function of supervision was said to be furnishing police expertise in situations that civilians might not fully appreciate:

> I remember when we were doing the transition from the police to civilian dispatchers, we had an officer in dis-

patch and actually, if we are going to have civilians there, an officer there supervising [them] worked very well. Because when the shit hit the fan, the officer directed, you do this and you do this and you do this because the officer in there knew what needed to be done, but for some reason the civilians are not in the mindset of what needs to be done.

The other side of the issue was said to be that "if you need someone to stand over them and tell them when to tie their shoes, then they probably shouldn't even be there." A more conservative response, therefore, to any deficits in police expertise was more training, because, "Once they complete their initial training, there really is no training for them and they get to a certain stage and that is it, and then they plateau and sometimes even drop."

To the suburban officers' credit, they did not confine their discussion to a litany of miscellaneous grievances. Many of the problems of dispatching, for example, were judged not to be the dispatchers' personal fault. Thus, dispatchers were not expected to know the strengths and limitations of individual officers. The dispatchers would know in principle that "you don't want to give a shooter to a guy that won't know how to handle a shooter, you want to give him the barking dog call," but they would not be able to assess the capabilities of officers. In some respects, officers would always have to compensate for the limited knowledge of dispatchers:

> We hear certain calls go out that just get the whole shift gravitating because we know that we are not getting half the information, we just know we are not, so we are going to cover it because there is a high probability that it is going to be a shooter. So we get enough people there to cover, so that no one hopefully gets hurt.

The group expressed awareness of the fact that the dispatchers would have grievances of their own. This meant that one ought not to think in terms of problem dispatchers, but of problems involving dispatchers. One of the officers said, semifacetiously,

> Well, I am sure that if you had the supervisors in here that we would be the problem, and I am sure that if you had the dispatchers in here, we would be the problem, too. Fortunately, we know we are not.

The officers credited some individual dispatchers with being helpful and emphasized that they were not questioning the motivation and dedication of the dispatchers as a group:

> GM1: They come in, they do their job. They don't come in with the attitude that I am coming in and I am just coming in and I am going to do my 8 hours, and I am going to sit in the corner, and I am going to talk to my friends on the telephone or my boyfriend or my girlfriend, and I am going to play a couple of computer games, and I am going to read this here magazine.
> GM2: Jay, cops do that too.
> GM1: Oh, they do, I said that already.

Given the definition of the problem as one affecting two groups of stout-hearted men (and women) of goodwill who might have understandable differences to resolve, conciliatory, collaborative solutions were deemed appropriate. Officers and dispatchers could be convoked in congenial conclaves to discuss problems of mutual interest, in subservience to common goals:

> I will tell you why we are hot on this, and we got a lot of input on this, because it is something that we can actually get some product. Yeah, we can solve this problem . . . it comes down to, like, how to make my job safer and better and what I need to get my job done, well, I got a lot to say about that, everybody could give their input on that. . . . Is anything more important than us getting home safe at the end of our tour of duty? Nothing is more important than that.

The officers concluded that if there were working-level input into organizational problems such as dispatching, the department would benefit from the constructive solutions that would inevitably emerge. As a case in point, the officers mentioned problems of radio communication they had observed:

> GM1: The importance of the radio can't be underestimated, it is almost more important to have a radio than it is to have a gun.
> GM2: Oh, absolutely, that is your lifeline to call for help. You know, we have all these little problems that take forever to solve them. This could be the best department in the state, or one of the best, so easy it is right there to take. We are not far off, we just have all these little things that were really never solved. They are Band-Aided or they take forever to repair.

Rank-and-File Problem Solving

The city officers saw the principal action implication of the survey data analysis as

> a process or procedure that maybe [one] could suggest that instead of attacking one of these [problems] specifically, you might be able to come up with a process that people could buy into that would say, "Here is any problem, what should be the channels to address that particular problem today?"

In furtherance of grass-roots problem-solving efforts, officers could individually research solutions and develop expertise that could benefit the organization:

> There is a lot of stuff that we can do like that. Decide who is the best at doing this, as far as, if Greenville is the best with cars, if Middletown is best with computers, see what they do, mirror what they do, and fix their little problems and then you're the best.

* * *

Just as an example, we have dispatchers, one is phenomenal with the computer, but he is not utilized whatsoever, went to school for computers and he is not utilized. If we utilized a lot of people's potential, J and C are car geniuses, utilize that, B is a gun genius, utilize that, you know what I mean. . . . L has done a lot for us, you can't deny him that. I think he deserves accolades for the range, him and whoever got us that. . . . I am just saying that if we use people's potential, instead of worrying about who is going to look better than me, that's important, that is what makes you better, we are going to mirror who does what best, fix their little imperfections and you're the best.

* * *

You also have to be on the same page and realize that in the end we are all on the same page, we are all in the same police department. You know, everybody should strive not to excel themselves, but to excel the department, and so, the entire department looks great. The whole entire organization—and that goes from everything to appearance of cars, the quality of work.

When the city chief of police joined the workshop session of his subordinates, he encountered a set of constructive suggestions and a high level of enthusiasm for reform. The message of the officers to the chief was that they would be pleased to try to help him solve departmental problems if he were willing to create vehicles for their participation.

This result presented to the chief is not serendipitous, nor was it surprising. Proposals for constructive change are the expected products of the process of data feedback. Surveys in organizations delineate and illuminate problems perceived or experienced by members of the organization. Feedback sessions relating to such surveys invite group members to analyze any problems they have identified and lead them to ask whether the problems can be solved. Almost invariably, ideas for responsive interventions emerge. Administrators in organizations that have been surveyed in action research projects such as ours can avail themselves of the opportunity thus provided to implement data-based solutions that are recommended to them.

Postscript

Presenting the results of our research has centered on data from the larger, more heterogeneous department, because our study in this setting posed some interesting questions about differences in perceptions of different groups of police officers. In this chapter primarily about the data feedback process in the city department, however, this coverage is relatively brief, because the session was confined to a review of inferences one might draw from responses to the survey. The "action" portion of the model was not heavily invoked, given that prospective actors remained to be nominated and appointed by the city.

The administration that took office in the city department did review the study, both the research and results, and expressed reservations about its validity and import. To the extent to which the report did have impact, it was primarily and exclusively by confirming a resolve to intensify efforts to ameliorate race-related conflicts in the department.

The suburban session did, however, produce follow-up activity. The chief who attended the session reported that he was impressed by the discussion and sensitized to the need for reform. He followed this up by arranging for a presentation to his management team and hiring an organizational development consultant to initiate reforms in his department. Although these reforms did not take place under our auspices, the study provided an incentive for the intervention and contributed to its timing. The content of the discussion also led the chief to undertake actions in relation to the court system, which had become the subject of acrimonious debate. Moreover, the president of the officer union, who had been a key player in the project and a principal contributor to the feedback session, participated in organizational reform. The process is ongoing, and it is difficult to dissect the nature and extent of our contribution to it. To the extent to which reform is usefully informed by knowledge, we can probably claim that the data feedback sessions we have described helped lay a foundation for responsive interventions.

7

Actualization and Stress

In policing today, we see not only more diversity and its attendant strains (see chapter 5), but also other changes that can affect the motivation and morale of officers. The most important of these changes have to do with philosophical realignments that expand the officer's job. In theory, the police profession is becoming more professional. Officers can exercise more discretion, acquire new knowledge, refine their skills, and contribute more substantially to the communities they serve.

The goal of policing becomes redefined as the solution of problems, rather than the one-on-one response to disruptive incidents (Goldstein, 1980). Arrests are only one option the police can exercise, and a choice of appropriate responses must be made mindfully. In other words, officers must become students of societal problems to help address them. They must also work with a variety of partners in efforts to solve problems.

To the extent to which this type of theory is enacted, it offers the greatest rewards to officers who are "self-actualizers" in Maslow's sense of the term, which is "to become everything that one is capable of becoming" (1970, p. 92). For such men and women, the new knowledge they acquire, their honed expertise, and their expanded horizons should offer very special satisfaction. Police work should become personally motivating to some officers in the same sense as "a musician must make music, an artist must paint, a poet must write, if he is to be ultimately at peace with himself" (p. 91).

If such is to occur, the police organization must obviously change to facilitate and support actualization—to provide opportunities for the acquisition of knowledge and the freedom to apply it. As Goldstein (1980) noted about officers engaged in problem solving, "It follows that increasing their involvement in identifying problems hinges on creating an environment within the organization that is supportive of problem-oriented policing" (p. 75).

In relation to motivation and morale, the problem-oriented enterprise is thus a two-edged sword. On the one hand, offering officers the opportunity to participate in problem solving can lead to greatly enhanced work satisfaction—especially among those who find self-development intrinsically rewarding. On the other hand, if consistent organizational support is not forthcoming, problem-oriented officers can feel that they have been set up for disillusionment.

The danger is real because police organizations are frequently procedurally inflexible. By the same token, policing is a demand-oriented profession, apt to redirect operational goals (and consequent definitions of assignments) as new priorities are set. Moreover, whatever trends exist within police agencies may not be univocal. As Goldstein (1980) pointed out, "Police agencies have long been notorious for urging rank-and-file officers to do one thing, while rewarding them for doing something else" (p. 163). A community police officer explained to me once during an interview how he was recruited to his assignment. He said about his chief,

> He was pounding a banner that said community policing, but in private to the guys, he was saying, "Look, I don't believe in this any more than you do. It failed in New York City. It failed there, it's going to fail here. But let's just get it out, you know, and let it fail so that we can get on with life. . . ." Then he changed his tune a little bit, and [said], "Well, that's not exactly what I meant. How about if I do this for you, you do that for me?"

This contextual problem is sufficiently important to warrant exploratory study. To this end, we approached some officers (mostly of supervisory rank) in a police agency who were nominated as actualizers by their peers. Each officer had been defined as a problem-oriented expert who had developed an impressive area of specialization, sometimes with substantial support. As a downside, each officer had at some juncture been discouraged from continuing to pursue his or her specialized activities to the desired degree.

The department in which the case studies were compiled is an enlightened and sophisticated one, in which supervisors support knowledge-based activities and value educational attainment. As an indication, the department's leadership not only authorized our interviews, but also invited feedback about issues that arise when one develops and utilizes specialists in problem areas of policing.

I conducted lengthy semistructured interviews, and I present excerpts of these interviews that highlighted experiences of self-defined stress. In each case, I center on junctures in the narrative having to do with the discontinuance of support for the specialized activities of the officer in question.

Stressful Experiences

To set a context for these junctures, I assumed them to be historical. As far as I knew, none of the officers had seriously considered retirement, and none showed evidence of burnout. Each had been described as a highly respected member of the force who effectively contributed to its mission. Each came across as motivated, enthusiastic, and dedicated. Each maintained vestiges of former interests, although with varying degrees of bitterness and traces of nostalgia.

The format of my presentation requires a brief justificatory comment. Interview excerpts are customarily framed by appropriate explanatory text highlighting the themes that the excerpts are presumed to illustrate. I have opted here to transcribe three sets of interview extracts, in sequence, without interspersed commentary. The sequences are intended to relay retrospective accounts of careers or career segments. In these accounts, the nuances of individual perception and feelings appear to me to matter a great deal. My hope is that the reader can get an uncontaminated sense of the intense involvement, commitment, and dedication reflected in the narratives, and of the disappointment and frustration they ultimately convey.

A perspective I hope the reader may glean relates to the chronologies that unfold. Actualizers are made, not born. Actualization is instigated through training that takes hold through grass-roots scholarship, application of knowledge in action, and networking. Opportunities to experience self-efficacy by deploying knowledge are essential. Networking is important because it provides collegiality and sustenance. When a person functions as an expert in a nonacademic setting, this places collegiality at a distance but enhances its value and significance. Networks update one's knowledge, reinforce one's commitment, and provide psychological support. A network acquires added salience where institutional support is weak. Where resistances came to be seen as overwhelming, stress may be shared among network members. The ultimate problem to be faced is whether one can retain some vestige of one's professional function and identity.

The Expert in Psychological Profiling

> SP1:   I had more work [that involved psychological profiling consultation] than I could handle, and it was a matter of trying to prioritize the workload.... Trying to work an enormous amount of cases, put quality into every case, and trying to contribute to every case investigation whether or not you came up with a suspect. You may not always do that, but you make some contribution upon every instance of getting a request for help. That was challenging and satisfying . . . very fulfilling for me.

> HT: Can you remember at that time how many hours a week you would be putting in?

> SP1:   Hundreds.

HT: Hundreds?

SP1:   Seven days a week. That's not an exaggeration. I think that's probably the experience that everybody who got involved with [psychological profiling] had ... Almost all your thinking, waking moments you were thinking about some case. That's really what the case involved—was thinking about it.

HT: So, this was a really consuming enterprise?

SP1:   Very much so.

* * *

SP1:   I thought we were going forward. There was optimism that maybe we would be able to expand, and maybe I could share what I knew with other people and clone myself so that my caseload of, say, 250 cases a year. ... I would like to do 50 and have other people do 50 ... and I think in the beginning there was good intention to have done that. Somewhere along the way, it lost priority. ... I could tell by the reaction of my executive superiors. ... They had no idea what I was able to do or what my commitment was supposed to be to outside agencies or to our own agency. That lack of knowledge began to hurt me. They started pulling in the reins and my activities out there working cases, and I became very frustrated in that I was being inhibited from doing the best I could do.

HT: Now, how do you think they saw you?

SP1:   One particular colonel would probably tell you that I was a rogue.

HT: A what?

SP1:   A rogue. R-O-G-U-E.

HT: What would he mean by that?

SP1:   Overly independent, unsupervised, loose cannon ...

HT: A loose cannon.

SP1:   Because there was no one who knew what I did.

My supervisor could not supervise me, because he had no idea how I did what I did or what I did, and typically I was on the road, 8 to 10 months a year working in the field with investigators without my first-line supervisor there looking over my shoulder as to what I was doing.

HT: And so the fact that you couldn't be supervised in the conventional sort of way, that would bother him?

SP1:   I think it would bother him because I did have a great deal of at least perceived independence, and they would never really know what I was doing even though what I was doing was probably working 18 hours a day, 7 days a week.

HT: So, you were very highly motivated, dedicated, and spending twice as much time on the job as the average member of the organization, and you were being seen as not subserving them, so to speak.

SP1:   In a sense, I was definitely not at that point in time, particularly traditionally subservient.

HT: So you're talking factually subservient—in a sense that there was no way of fitting you into the chain of command? You are not saying that your attitudes were nonsubservient? That is, that you were in a sense manifesting some rebelliousness or something?

SP1:   I think it could have been perceived that way, but what in fact I think I was doing, if I had an opinion about how I thought a case should go, I would not hesitate to speak my mind. Where now, in the position I am in now, I take orders. You don't question orders any more; I mean, that's what I do. Then, if I was convinced that things should go a certain way, then I would express my opinion as strongly as possible and try to give reasons for why we should be doing things this way, which from their perspective may not have been traditional, so therefore, they were not understood. But from my perspective, having the experience base, in a nontraditional area now, it made nothing but perfect sense to me but no sense to them, perhaps. And so there came an extended period of conflict. It gradually got to be greater and greater.

HT: Now, when you say conflict, you mean that people

behind your back are getting disgruntled or do you mean that some actual verbal exchanges took place?

SP1: Verbal exchanges. I don't think there was much behind the back. If there was, I don't know about it to this day.

HT: So, this was actually face-to-face conflict.

SP1: Yes, I would have telephone calls. On one particular case I was out in R. It was a long-term case. It was a serial killer case. Since I had done a good serial killer case out there before, they'd asked me to come out there and look at this one. I was out there for a long time. It was hard work, and a lot of questions were being asked as to how come it's taking him so long? I was called back to division headquarters at least twice and asked, "Why are you there so long? What are you doing? What kind of progress is being made? You are giving them too much.". . . And my response was, "We have girls getting killed out here, and how much is too much?" I mean, this is an important case. Probably, at that time, it was the most important murder case in the state, whether it was publicized or not. It was within my area of expertise, and that is where I felt I should have been. I stayed there as long as I could until they pulled me. They actually withdrew me from the case.

HT: Did they pull you before your time, so to speak?

SP1: I should have stayed longer. . . .

HT: Now, would this be a sample of what you meant when you said they were inhibiting you?

SP1: There came a time when I was told that I could not work a case unless it was cleared specifically by a specific colonel. I was very frustrated by that because in my mind I felt he had no sense of how to decide what case I could work and couldn't work based on what I knew. . . . I didn't feel that those decisions should be arbitrarily made by a colonel . . . it was frustrating for me to have somebody else making decisions about the cases I should work when they had no, absolutely no, expertise in what I did.

HT: Now, let's think about this a bit. You are a member of the State Police, which is a hierarchical, centralized organization.

SP1:   That is correct!

HT: . . . and you were a cog in this machine.

SP1:   That is correct.

HT: And you are telling me you are feeling uncomfortable because a colonel who is distinctly higher up in the hierarchy . . .

SP1:   The word is not "uncomfortable."

HT: How would you describe your feelings?

SP1:   As time progressed, it went from frustration to anger to depression where I just couldn't do it anymore.

HT: So, you are saying, if I can't pick my cases, then I'm not going to do any?

SP1:   Well, no, it didn't really come to that. There were other things involved, but that was certainly one aspect of it. It was frustrating for me . . . you're a psychologist. You probably understand this a lot better than a lay person, but it was frustrating for me for somebody to tell me which cases I could best work when they had no idea what it was I even did.

HT: So, instead of spending your nights up suffering from insomnia because you are ruminating about a case, you are now spending your nights up eating your heart out because this colonel . . .

SP1:   Yes, because I'm not up with insomnia working a case. Ironic, isn't it? What ended up happening was, I would not be able to work the cases I was told not to do on duty. I had to work them off duty.

* * *

SP1:   And people were asking me, "Then, why do you continue doing [psychological profiling work]? You're spending a fortune of your own money, you have no private life, you have no personal time because you have dedicated yourself to this, you're getting yelled at more and more doing what they thought was good work and being very dedicated." And they said, "Why are you still doing this?"

HT: When you are not being appreciated?

SP1:   Appreciated not only in the knowledge sense of the word. It was not appreciated because people did not understand what it was I did or how much effort had to go into doing what I did.

HT: So, you would almost be swimming against the tide?

SP1:   It became that way, and that's not an experience that you need to make. It's happened to other people who are trained in this application who have gone back to their agencies.

HT: Really?

SP1:   Yes.

HT: But this was interfering with your life? That is, so to speak, what had been a joy sort of lost its attraction?

SP1:   It was the frustration of knowing that you were being kept back from maximizing the skills that you were developing. They were constantly in the developmental stage. You would always be growing.

* * *

SP1:   It was eating me up. I really felt that this whole application, this whole premise, in the beginning had great expectations and great promise. It could be developed to the nth degree. At one point in time [I began] to realize how much promise and potential there was in this application, in looking forward into continually developing this, and bringing other people on board, teaching them how to do it and sending them out, I didn't care who they worked for. It could be any PD; it didn't matter. This is a good technique, this is a good application. We can arrest a lot of bad guys using this application. Over time then, finding out that, that light had been turned down and gradually turned off, for me I just couldn't deal with that. All that promise was taken away; it was wasted. I was angry. I was angry that that light had been turned down and turned off.

HT: Now that's a pretty eloquent way of putting it. Obviously, there is a tremendous amount of disappointment here. I mean, there was this promise and you saw all of this potential and all this opportunity. Not only doesn't that materialize, but you see yourself increasingly stymied, but you still have a limited amount of scope to do some of this. You are saying that you are feeling so upset at what is happening that you essentially take the position, "I'm not going to do any of this under these auspices, right?"

SP1:   Right! The reason for that is, again, if I am doing this, if this is my job to do this, and they are telling me I can only do it halfway or you can do it your way on your own time, I know what my decision is going to be. I know that I will be working 24 hours a day working cases, when really I should be getting support and resources to do that and I'm not going to get it. So, I've got to make this not my job anymore, or else I'm going to incinerate. I'm going to take too much on myself, put too much of myself and too much of my resources and my own time into this, the only way I can get out from my own self-created dilemma is to just not be in this world anymore.

* * *

HT: You would do it [pursue psychological profiling work] over again, wouldn't you? Even knowing what would happen?

SP1:   I think so. Things aren't all that tragic. I just had a life adjustment. I've had a life adjustment, and it's not like a tragic end. I just changed jobs.

HT: But you are willing to compromise, aren't you? In the sense that you are really good at something you are not doing. What you are now doing, probably can be done by other people just as well?

SP1:   Perhaps, can be done just as well by a chimpanzee,

I guess. But my quality of life has gone up. My stress level has gone down. I'm probably physically healthier. So, there have been some positive returns.

The Expert on Child Molestation

SP2: I'm not saying that I am the Mother Theresa of this. I'm not saying that. What I'm saying is there aren't too many of me around. People will go, "Well, you know that's quite egotistical saying something like that." Well, you know what? When you are the only fish in the pond, you are looking around for another fish. You'd really like to know if there is one in here, and I'm not seeing another fish. Now, if there is another one hiding under a log, come on out. I want to meet you. When I went to that advanced seminar with the FBI, I thought that I died and went to heaven. I was sitting in a room with 51 other people that understood every word I was saying. It was like, Wow, I didn't have to go into a training session every time I opened my mouth. They told me that there were people there that were in [child molestation work] as long as or longer than I was. They told me that this is going to happen to you, this is going to happen to you, this is going to happen to you, this is going to happen to you, and you know, it did!

HT: Would you say that these other folks who have developed the same area of expertise in their police agencies have suffered pretty much the same fate that you have? None of them, in a sense, are fully supported?

SP2: Right. I know for a fact that the last time I was in New York City for a pedophile unit, there were five people in the whole New York City Pedophile Unit. That took care of five boroughs. You can't do that, but when somebody asks the hierarchy of the New York City Police Department, "Do you have a pedophile unit?" "Oh yeah, we have a very active one." Sure they are active. You have five people working their asses off because they don't have any choice about it.

HT: And the reason you think they only have five people, is because they are ambivalent about the area?

SP2:   I think they need to be able to say they have a unit.

HT: But they are not really fully convinced that this is important?

SP2:   You said it.

HT: Is that just—to get some closure on this—because it is not really mainline police work or viewed as main-line police work, or because it is slightly unsavory or suspect?

SP2:   I think that it is all of the above. When you go and look at statistics of sex crime arrests. . . . I did this at sem-inars . . . you ask law enforcement people, "How many people handle a tremendous amount of rape cases?" You see the hands go up. "How many sexual abuse cases?" You see the hands go up. Then you say to them, "Okay, now, my next question is the important one. The majority of your rape cases, the majority of your sexual abuse cases, most of your sodomy cases, are they children cases or adult cases? If they are children cases, please, or if they are adult cases, raise your hands." The majority. You want to see hands go up. The next one is children, you see all hands go up. Now what or why is the resistance within the law enforcement community, or is it not just the law enforcement community? Is the law enforcement community no more reflective of the attitude on this type of crime [than] general society? I think they are one. I think they are almost parallel.

* * *

SP2:   I understand that [child molestation] is not a pop-ular topic, it is not a popular subject. It's not very "po-licey," so to speak. Okay? It's not very glamorous; it's really that gutter of society. I can understand why some-one in law enforcement who is a policy maker, or in a decision position, would that person really be any dif-ferent from someone in my audience? They don't want to hear it, they don't want to talk about it, they don't want to see it. One thing that I noticed in my travels, when you are working prostitution, child pornography, early on when you went to different police agencies, no matter where you went, that topic was treated the same internally. They head down into the basement as far away as you could get from the rest of all the other activities, stuffed in a little tiny room that was as far away as they could get you. That's no different from the way it's treated by society.

* * *

SP2:   You can train a chimpanzee to do narcotics. Money, dope, dope, money. Yep, a little bit dangerous at the time of the assist, at the time of the switch when the money and the drugs come together. Very dangerous right then, because he is worrying about you ripping off his drugs and you are worrying about him ripping off your money. All right? But if you got a line of bullshit, I've proved it to people, even at my age that I can still buy drugs. If you have a line of shit, you can go buy drugs. That's police-y. That's very "cop-y" and whoa! Very gross, wow, narcotics. To have a little 7-year-old girl sitting there twisting her arms like she's going to turn into a pretzel because her father's molesting her, these big, burly cops, they can't do this shit. So you know what? There has got to be something wrong with you if you are doing it. If there is something wrong with you, I'm not going to give you too much of a leash here.

* * *

HT: So, that in a sense it almost sounds like, they are discouraging you.

SP2:   I refuse to be discouraged. It's because I understand. I understand why the resistance. If there is in fact really a resistance. Maybe there are other things that are more important. I am not the only act in town, and I understand that.

HT: So, it could simply be that because this area is important to you, that you feel it ought to get more attention than every other person who takes an area seriously?

SP2:   That would be selfish, saying something like that. I think that if the powers that be would just sit and analyze, they would see that there is a need here—a really genuine need here.

HT: Now why couldn't you convince them of that?

SP2:   Because [child molestation] is the last taboo. There is very little difference from my hierarchy than that zillion population out there. It's the last taboo. Nobody wants to hear about it, speak about it, talk about it.

* * *

SP2:   I actually was told that a certain somebody said, "Get rid of that child crap, they need more on organized crime."

HT: Now, when you got down to one hour [of training time], you decided that this was insufficient.

SP2:   I just went and said, "This is ludicrous! Why? I can't do it." Now, being the stubborn Irish-German boy that I am, I said, "Here is what I'm going to do. I will come for the hour, but I want to do it Wednesday night, the last period of the day."

HT: So, "if they want to stay on, that's fine with me," right?

SP2:   Now these are men staying on their own time.

HT: So you are still going strong at 11:00 at night?

SP2:   Yes, sir, I was. Then they told me to stop doing that. Okay? Think of what I am saying. The cops want more, but somebody else didn't want it.

HT: There must have been more than curtailing your academy presentations?

SP2:   The shutdown was around every time I was making the turn around the corner. I was getting resistance.

* * *

SP2:   How many boy toys do we need? How many helicopters do you need flying around making a lot of noise? How many dogs do you need on a manhunt running up and down pissing on all the guardrails?

HT: So you are competing with helicopters and dogs when you are a person with some knowledge?

SP2:   Am I saying one is more important than the other? I'm not saying that. I'm just saying, "Who sits and analyzes this?" If it happens to be someone with a strong conviction, if [he or she says], "I don't want to listen to this kind of garbage!" That's where it stops. . . . About 12 years ago, a man had that much foresight and that much trust in me to say, "Okay, I'm going to give you your head start here. It's going to be up to you to pull it off."

HT: And in that respect . . .

SP2:   In that respect, I feel like a failure.

HT: Why?

SP2:   Because I never pulled it off. I never got the job to buy into what I was trying to tell them and to prove to them.

HT: Never buy into it fully. They did give you some scope for you to do some of this, but they didn't buy into it.

SP2:   That's what I feel.

The Expert on Responses to Emergencies

SP3:   It probably was a lot of pushing on my part, pleading, cajoling, and whatever you want to call it. It was showing and trying to get them to see that they had to do this [develop contingency plans and make provisions for emergencies], that they couldn't get away from it, and that there were repercussions involved.

HT: Is that still the full force of your argument—the price of noncompliance?

SP3:   Not just that, but we could look bad in our response. Everybody else out there is moving in this direction [coordinating responses to emergencies]. The days of us saying that we can do it by ourselves, alone, without the assistance of other people, is a conditioned mentality we've been in since 1917. We don't need this anymore, so what I did was foster the idea that we are moving in this direction anyway. We should be leaders of the group—right in front of the pack. If we have to interact with everybody else, we might as well be the most knowledgeable, experienced on the street out there.

* * *

HT: Had you convinced the people in [the organization] at that juncture? Do they come with you reluctantly?

SP3:   Always reluctantly. The key to any success I had was showing that I had more knowledge and more expertise than any of them. I'm the resident expert, and they had to do what I suggested. That's the way it worked. Is it a game? Yes, it is. Does it work? Yes, it does. I got away with it for 7 years. If I was the expert, did they test my expertise? Yes, they did. They ultimately saw that what I said was accurate and that there were penalties for noncompliance and what-have-you.

* * *

HT: Let me try to see whether I understand why this has been a sort of an uphill battle. I sense it has been an uphill battle.

SP3:   Always!

HT: That is, you are drawing attention to low probability events which have very serious consequences. The State Police is weighing the probabilities. So it isn't particularly concerned in investing a lot of money in something that has a one-in-one-thousand chance of occurring. Is that part of the reason for the reluctance? . . .

SP3:   Probabilities. Are they looking at it that way? Probably. Probably. Reluctance to do a program that would necessitate the use of resources, the use of money, use of time. Yes. We had an awful lot of initiatives on the stove, all of them cooking at the same time.

HT: And you are competing with them?

SP3:   Yes.

HT: At times did the result, as you are meeting resistance along the way, become painful or, you know, sort of ugly?

SP3:   It was probably the reason I ultimately left there. I got out because it was a continuous fight. There were always other initiatives. Also, it reached the point where I was promoted to captain. The expectations were that I would run multiple programs. I believe that I did, but I was ultimately told that I was spending too much time in emergency management.

HT: Too much time and energy on this?

SP3:   As far as emergency management, what the division should have done and I still believe they should do, is there should be a full-time individual devoted to emergency management issues. What the division's history is, they like to combine different issues.

* * *

HT: If one were to look at your own situation, one would say: "Well, you know, maybe you had to do a little convincing [to get emergency management policies adopted], but it doesn't look like you got hurt any." That is, they did put some resources at your disposal. They gave you the opportunity to go to all of these training situations. You got promoted. You wouldn't exactly be a case study of somebody who got the ax.

SP3:   No, but it could be so much better than it is. By continuously fighting getting to point Z, it's frustrating, it's irritating, it eventually reaches the point where you say, "Why am I hitting myself on the head? Why am I doing this?" I love what I do. I loved my involvement in this program, but when it started affecting me and my family, it's time to start to move on. What you need to understand about the hierarchy in the State Police is, particularly in division headquarters, there are multiple competing agendas. If my program doesn't fit into other programs, resources, commitment, or if endorsements or sponsorship does not occur—and every time there is a shift up here in the organization, I have to start the fight all over again. It eventually reached the point where I said, I can't fight anymore.

HT: How would you describe your state of mind at this point? Tired? Disgusted?

SP3:   At that point, tired, disgusted, irritated, frustrated, and any number of other conditions or whatever you want to call them. Have I given up on emergency management? No. I do it at a different level; I do it at my own level in the organization. I probably do it better than anybody on the job.

HT: You are still involved?

SP3:   Oh, yes. Yes. I attend all the state meetings, the conferences, the local meetings.

* * *

HT: Now they do have somebody who has taken [emergency management] over?

SP3:   Yes ... I ask him how frustrated he is, and he is frustrated. . . . Given the history of the institution, he will probably burn out. It's the way we do business. Every time there is a new promotion in-house, there is a new somebody on the executive board. It's the typical fight over again. "Why do we need this? Why are we doing this?"

HT: And you see this as partly being a competition for resources by people with different agendas?

SP3:   Yes.

* * *

SP3:   He has to do what I did—resort to chicanery, treachery, deception, and deceit. That's the bottom line.

HT: Really?

SP3:   He has to do whatever he possibly can to convince the powers that be down there that this is important, needed, and relevant.

HT: And at times you implied a sort of gloves-off, no-holds-barred game, right?

SP3:   Whatever works. There were a number of occasions where I was told that I exceeded my authority.
"Okay, I'll never do it again." It's a constant fight.

* * *

HT: Did you see this [reassignment] as a kind of opportunity to escape from what had become a difficult
situation?

SP3:   Yes. Yes. It was a different job. I needed a breath
of fresh air—a different environment—not a constant
fight. I have to say I have been much happier since.

HT: So, this was a stress reduction move?

SP3:   Oh, definitely a stress reduction move. Absolutely,
positively.

HT: Now, part of what you are saying is that you were
taking your job home with you, and this became increasingly frustrating, and somehow your family sensed from
your demeanor that . . .

SP3:   Yes. There were all of those issues—physical, social, psychological issues—we all bring the baggage
home. If you take your work seriously. If you take the
baggage home, it affects your family life. It's ridiculous.
You say "Why am I doing this?"

HT: It wasn't that some member of your family said to
you, "You really ought to find some different assignment?" They welcomed it?

SP3:   They welcomed the change. It was a significant
improvement. I was far, far happier.

HT: And it made them happy?

SP3:   Oh, yes. It's the issue that if any particular person
in the family isn't happy, not too many people are happy.

* * *

SP3:   It's ridiculous. For years I would go to work on
pass days, vacation, because I love the job. I'm results
oriented. I've always liked to succeed. I've been called a
pushy person. The bottom-line results are what I looked

for, and when I succeed, it's a good feeling. Does it drive me? Yeah.

HT: But you have in this case felt that you were succeeding in a good cause, right?

SP3:   Yes. Yes.

HT: Which you took very, very seriously, right?

SP3:   Yes.

HT: So, it wasn't just that it was nice to succeed, this success here matters a lot?

SP3:   In this endeavor, yes. Yes. I always believed that I should continue to learn. I build on what I have previously known. I am still involved.

* * *

SP3:   Well, this [emergency management job] has always been a learning experience. The whole job has always been a learning experience. I always wanted to be better. I always wanted to do the job better than anybody else. I always wanted to be able to see the results, to get the satisfaction, to be up front and see the whole picture. Not just me, but to move the group, move the agency; move everything together.

HT: But what you are now saying, though, is that if they had assigned you to training bomb-sniffing dogs or something else, the same process would have unfolded, right?

SP3:   Yes.

HT: You would now be a dog-sniffing expert, right?

SP3:   I was involved with dogs, horses, boats, aircraft, and all of that. It was fun, it was interesting. Was I as focused on that as I was emergency management? No.

HT: So there is something about emergency management services as such that got ahold of you?

SP3:   Yes. The potential is phenomenal. If we did it right, we could be a leader—a nationally recognized leader. If we did all of the things that needed to be done, we would have a program that would be absolutely phenomenal.

HT: You are almost salivating as you say it.

SP3:   Yes. The potential—that's probably the biggest frustration. People not seeing the potential.

* * *

HT: Do some of your counterparts tell stories that are similar to your experience, or are they by and large more successful in imbuing their agencies with their enthusiasm?

SP3:   Similar frustrations, similar experiences. All of them want to do a good job. All of them realize that it is an uphill, continuous battle with the bureaucracy. Just in the way this system works. Institutional memory regardless of agency is compounded, impacted, twisted, convoluted, or whatever the heck you want to call it. Promotions, transfers, retirements, and everything else— no memory: "Why do we need this?" "Why are we doing this?" "What does it cost?"

HT: The new person coming in always takes this stance toward every single activity under his auspices, or does he come in with an agenda of his own?

SP3:   Possibly both. He comes in and says, "I'm the new guy on the block. I've got to look at the whole operation." He's questioning everything.

HT: That doesn't mean that he is going to be hostile to everything?

SP3:   No. It doesn't, but it would be nice if the deck were stacked a little bit. It would be nice if there was some previous exposure so that he was familiar with the concepts, issues, and everything about the program so that he saw a need.

* * *

HT: I've talked to a number of very impressive people over the last few weeks who have been able to document

that some area would be very important and very exciting to expand within the State Police. They have, in some
instances, been closed down and in other instances been
discouraged. Can you think of some way to avoid this?
When somebody spends years developing an expertise
and a function within the State Police, that the structure
can keep this from being a continuous battle?

SP3:   Yes, I can. Whether anything would ever be implemented along those lines I would doubt. The State
Police is a full-service police agency. We respond to whatever the agency perceives to be the needs of the client.
Now, what has happened is our resources are limited.
They will always be limited. We cannot be everything to
everybody. What we have accepted and moved into—
and this is an acceptable standard—with almost every
program that we have ever gotten involved in, is we
have only paid initial attention to the issues, the programs, or whatever it is. Let me give you an example: a
bus accident. Multitudes of people are being injured or
killed. It's in the public eye; it's a public need, a public
demand, public sentiment. Something has to be done
about those huge buses rocketing down the road causing
injury and death.

   The State Police says, "We have to do something about
this." We develop a program to deal with that issue. We
implement the program. We spend a colossal amount of
time, money, resources, and everything else. We implement this program, the public see after the publicity that
we are actively involved. That we are out there solving
the problem. Therefore, the problem has gone away. As
soon as the public fervor is gone, the resources are si-
phoned off to other programs, other issues, other prominent things, and we are done in this.

HT: You have restated the problem very eloquently.
Now what is the solution?

The Principle of Disintegration

Any organization can squelch the enthusiasm it has engendered in its members. This paradox is a corollary of several

propositions that are axiomatic in industrial psychology. One is the expectation that if conditions are afforded for intrinsic work motivation—such as autonomy, responsibility, and opportunities for learning—high-quality productivity and high levels of job satisfaction will result. The key presumption is what Douglas MacGregor (1960) called the "principle of integration," which holds that motivated workers will contribute to the goals of their organization. The converse of this proposition is that organizations thrive through "the creation of conditions such that the members of the organization can achieve their own goals *best* by directing their efforts toward the success of the enterprise" (p. 316).

In practice, the road to integration of personal and organizational goals may be studded with land mines. For one, it takes two partners to integrate. Conservative workers may not be eager to take on more interesting work or work of greater complexity. Such workers may vociferously proclaim themselves overcommitted, ill-prepared, and undertrained. The unions representing the workers may demand adherence to rules that place obstacles in the way of reform. Conflict can result with respect to implementation details and so can frustration and stress. The greatest stress may result for the originator of innovation, as occurred with some of the early protagonists of community policing, who ended up losing their jobs because they were ahead of their time (Guyot, 1991).

More typically, resistance to change is less militant and more passive. Veteran members of organizations such as police departments may come to view announcements of reform with well-honed skepticism and with a firm conviction that "this too will pass." Police officers can become practiced virtuosos at sitting out revolutions in policing. New mission statements are routinely regarded as symbolic preludes to predictably evanescent developments. The locker room strategy is to reduce risk (and prevent stress) by staying off the bandwagon.

But there are always some officers who will respond to the availability of expanded opportunities because they are self-actualizers or careerists who are intent on making a favorable impression. In police departments, "community policing" is often the sum of such workers, congregated in small enclaves, and sometimes held in contempt by the rest of the force. Within the innovation ghettos, morale and esprit de corps tend to run exceptionally high as long as the department supports the innovation at issue.

Support for innovation may lapse for a variety of reasons. One is the fact that actualizers may actualize with excessive enthusiasm or in directions that are deemed controversial. The first experiments in community policing, which were called "team policing," were sometimes closed down after the teams running model neighborhoods proclaimed their unfettered autonomy. At other times, departments found the team concept less enticing when subsidies for initial demonstration experiments ran out.

Self-actualizing workers may even actualize in directions that are arguably antithetical to the goals of an organization. Police units have sometimes shown stupendous productivity at the expense of citizens being subjected to overenthusiastic ministrations.

In such cases, it becomes easy to conclude that autonomy inevitably leads to license and corruption. Intimidated managers (subservient to a "principle of disintegration") then restore control, circumscribe discretion, squelch initiative, and produce disillusionment. Officers—including those whose activities invited administrative backlash—are apt to conclude that any exercise of initiative (e.g., any "real police work") is unwelcome. Such officers invariably disseminate the proposition that the best stress prevention strategy is to do as little as possible.

On the organizational side of the equation, we have seen that the principle of integration of personal and organizational goals can be endangered by the lability of organizational goals. Our actualizers responded to challenges that were posed to them at specific junctures in time. At those junctures, they were furnished unique opportunities to develop their expertise and were supported in its exercise. Later, with changes in priorities, the same functions were devalued or downgraded in importance. The resulting message to the actualized worker is "Your vocational goals are no longer our goals, but don't take this personally." This message may sound routine to the supervisors who send it, but it poses a serious problem for the officers, whose valued priorities have not changed. Actualization is not a process that can be turned on and off like a faucet. This is so because the source of satisfaction is always the content of the work itself. And one cannot tell the worker that "the work you are doing is not as important as it used to be," because this is not an empirical fact. The proposition becomes even more implausible (and offensive) when the person who advances it is a generalist supervisor who is not sold on the value of work appreciated by his or her predecessors.

In summarizing the experience that included the interviews I have excerpted, I noted that "a problem the organization must clearly consider is how one can develop a specialist without setting him or her up for disappointment when his or her skills are in reduced demand. In the words of a police colleague, 'When they go out on a limb of specialization, it can be cut off behind them.'" Part of the problem can possibly be faced at its inception. Before a new expert is unleashed, one can assess the importance that one assigns to the problem that is to be addressed and the likelihood of one's continued interest in the problem. In police departments, such assessments can be communicated to the problem-oriented officer. One can also reconfirm one's continued commitment to the principle of integration. In theory, one ought not to unleash any actualizers unless one can provide them with continuity of support for their professional development.

Unfortunately, what is prescribed in theory is rarely done on a sustained basis in practice. Universities are virtually the only organizations that accord unlimited license to their denizens, who call this privilege "academic freedom" and tend to take it for granted.

Policing is a profession that is almost forced to advertise tight supervision as an organizational attribute. Where there is a publicized incident of questionable or unacceptable behavior by "poorly supervised" officers, managerial careers are cut short in the service of top-down "accountability." This occurs despite the fact that it is virtually impossible to physically supervise what officers do. Where disgruntled police officers allege (as they sometimes do) that "you're damned if you do and damned if you don't," they are referring to behavior that is singled out for attention when most of their behavior is unavailable to scrutiny.

Nowadays, leaders of police organizations are frequently schooled in public administration and are cognizant of the motivating potential of permissive or supportive leadership. By the same token, they have to operate within a hallowed paramilitary tradition. Moreover, appointed police leaders feel vulnerable to repercussions that can eventuate if a subordinate offends public or political sensibilities. The result can be a mostly enlightened regime which engages in occasional autocratic moves where circumstances seem to call for them. Such regimes might inspire caution in subordinates, but for officers to be forewarned is not necessarily to be forearmed.

Our interviewees came to assume that the obvious value of the work they were doing ought to ensure its continued support. Where this assumption was predictably disconfirmed, they struggled to find explanations for resistance or opposition beyond that of the vagaries of organizational supports. They felt discouraged, disappointed, and disillusioned and defined such junctures as stress. Although they handily regrouped, a residue of bitterness remained.[1]

It would be nice to think that some formula existed to prevent such contingencies from arising. Unfortunately, the most obvious solution—not to create specialists in the first place —is a nonstarter. For one, professional police organizations need specialists. In the department under study, several new fields of expertise were being created to address emerging problems, in the course of our interviews. New opportunities

---

[1] In the interviews I have excerpted, all of the officers indicated that they were comfortable with their current assignments. But when I attempted to circulate a draft of this chapter for approval 30 months later, I discovered that all three of the officers had retired.

were arising for officers to gain and deploy new knowledge. Other considerations aside, it would be a disservice to these incipient officer-specialists to argue against the enrichment of their jobs on the grounds that this could "set them up" for disillusionment.

Most to the point, the curtailment of specialty areas would be a disservice not only to the officers, but also to their profession. To limit the development of expertise is to invite historical regression.[2] If policing is to change, the jobs of officers must change. Should occupational stress be a corollary of job enrichment, one must deal with it as a fact of organizational life. It is arguably a small price to pay for the progress one attains along the way.

---

[2] In alluding to areas of "expertise," I refer to substantiated knowledge acquired through academic preparation and/or formal training, and buttressed through voracious reading and disciplinary cross-fertilization. In policing, as in other fields, there are areas of self-defined expertise that lack these attributes.

A salient risk lies in equating "street experience" with solid documentation. Although experience can be a valuable adjunct to systematic knowledge (and may usefully flesh out bare-bones data to accord them meaning and substance), invoking "street experience" as authority can serve to perpetuate time-honed stereotypes and cherished mythology. This process is reinforced where myths are shared, making it more entrenched, obdurate, and susceptible to perpetuation.

8

Critical-Incident Stress

During the course of our study, a police officer was killed on duty in the city police department in which we were working. The officer and his partner were gunned down without warning while on patrol; the partner survived. The assailant proved to be a teenager, and the officer had, ironically, been noted for his work with youngsters in classroom settings and elsewhere. A friend recalled that the officer had told him that "the thing he liked best was helping people, especially kids. Public service meant a lot to him. Whether it was police work or teaching in the city schools . . . he liked to help keep kids on a straight path."

The city was literally in mourning, with flags flown at half-mast and donations pouring in for the officer's family. The police department was devastated. The funeral cortege of more than 500 police cars stretched over miles of road, and thousands of police officers from several departments stood pressed shoulder to shoulder in a convention hall accommodating only 2,500. The stressful nature of the occasion was documented in our survey. "Officer killed in the line of duty" came up time and again as a salient stress experience.[1]

---

[1]Gentz (1994) conducted two surveys relating to critical-incident stress

Besides the police officer's bereaved family, another griev-
ing person struggled with his feelings of loss and mourning:
the officer's partner, who had been shot in the leg. In the
hospital, he confessed to reporters that he could not manage
to sleep, waking often during the night and going over the
shooting incident repeatedly in his mind. He said that he was
much less concerned about his physical recovery than about
the state of his mind.

That officer's experience is of the kind in which any defi-
nitional quibbles are inappropriate. In the words of Richard
Blak (1990), "it would appear that certain tragic events are
so dramatic, shocking and disturbing to our collective psy-
ches that we agree that they are 'stressful' and therefore 'critical incidents'" (p. 40). The most widely cited critical incidents involve shootings—either of officers or by officers—
but other experiences, involving pain, suffering, or death, are
of equivalent concern. A standard list of occasions qualifying
as critical incidents even includes witnessing a fellow officer
taking a bribe, involvement in hostage negotiation, and the
experience of "suspension or threat of dismissal" (p. 42).
Gentz (1990) pointed out that "definitions often include references to an event in which an officer is subject to a sudden
serious jeopardy: perhaps a serious threat to his existence or
well-being, or the existence or well-being of another person."
He noted that

> other descriptions include a significant element of loss,
> such as death or serious injury of a partner, loss of a
> physical ability, a loss in terms of a major disruption of
> the officer's values, or loss of basic assumptions about
> his environment, or those who live in it. (p. 175)

and reported that "the death or serious injury of a fellow police officer"
ranked as the most frequently cited traumatic event. The reactions of officers to the news of such an incident included a sense of slow motion, a
sense of detachment, tunnel vision, an adrenaline surge, crying, tremors,
profuse perspiration, dizziness, involuntary laughter, extreme fatigue,
headaches, disbelief, anger, fear, guilt, elation, shame, preoccupation, sad-
ness, and depression. These were first reactions, and some officers also
experienced continuing or delayed symptoms.

For Gentz, the essential element of a definition is that a critical incident must be "an event requiring an extraordinary degree of adaptation by the individual" (p. 175).

The above ruminations were offered at a conference, Critical Incidents in Policing, hosted by the Federal Bureau of Investigation (FBI) at its headquarters in Quantico, Virginia (Reese, Horn, & Dunning, 1990). One of the participants at this conference, Gold (1990), contributed an essay that eloquently focused on the experiential component of critical incidents. She wrote in part,

> Each loss is different and each loss is the worst. Suffering enters the depth of our being and that is a place into which analysis cannot go because words are inadequate, they cannot explain this loss, this ache. In the world of the grieving, words have no power. . . .
>
> Losses cannot be prepared for. Even when death is anticipated or imminent as in catastrophic disease or terminal illness, it is impossible to comprehend the impact of the loss before the loss actually takes place. Emptiness and loneliness are feelings that do not come into fruition until they have been felt. Some empty spaces can never be filled and some spaces that do get filled forever feel empty. . . .
>
> We search for meaning from the pain and emptiness we feel. We try to make sense of why. But this is beyond what we can comprehend. This makes no sense. . . .
>
> Change precludes security. Moment to moment, life unfolds as it should with a rhyme and reason that serves a purpose even if that purpose eludes us. We suffer because we dwell on what could have been, what ought to have been, what might have been. The possibilities of the if-onlys are endless. What we expected, did not happen; what happened, we did not expect. We feel entitled to more. There is so much chaos, so much confusion, so much suffering; we ache for how it used to be, how we thought it would always be. . . .
>
> Yesterday is forever beyond our control, as are its circumstances. No matter how hard we wish, how much we plead or cajole, how much and what we are willing

> to give as part of our bargaining powers, life will not be returned. We cannot undo or bring back yesterday. As we have no control over its events, so is our mastery of tomorrow out of our bounds. (pp. 182–184)

Such experiences must be worked through, and if the person is willing to share this process with another human being, the task can be facilitated. There are many prescriptions for the assistance to be provided at such junctures, but the key ingredient of most is empathic listening. This fact may be obfuscated in some instances by labels attached to the process, such as "ventilating" (which sounds almost pejoratively irrational) and "debriefing" (which sounds very rational and judgmental), but the process is Rogerian (in the sense that we equate helpful listening with Carl Rogers). Klein (1990) described the stance as "something to the effect of: 'I don't know exactly what you are going through but I would just like to be here to listen to you.'" He noted that "you provide a safe, confidential and non-judgmental environment for the person to get in touch with the feelings and the emotions" (p. 240). Because the client—typically an officer involved in an incident such as a shooting—tends to wallow in endless replays, the listener encourages or facilitates a systematic ("frame-by-frame") narrative. The process of step-by-step retelling and reliving is designed to restore perspective and lead to acceptance. According to Klein, officers must accept that their actions in a crisis were

> governed by information they had at the time, and nothing more. If, for example, they had realized that the suspect was a juvenile, that it was the wrong person, or that [he was] not armed, they might have taken a different course of action. (p. 241)

If irreversible errors were in fact committed, the task presumably is one of learning to live with the knowledge of one's occasional fallibility and its tragic consequences.

Police Crisis Intervention

Ameliorative responses to crisis situations are most obviously called for in natural disasters, where the lives of many human beings are cataclysmically disrupted. The concept of crisis intervention historically originated in the realization that psychological assistance as well as material assistance is called for in the aftermath of disasters. Later, more systematic definitions of the modality (such as those of Caplan, 1964; Kardiner & Spiegel, 1947; and Lindemann, 1944) introduced several conceptual elements that are commonly accepted today. One of these is the desirability of intervening as soon after the crisis as is practicable. This requisite undergirds the creation of specially trained "intervention teams," which become available for instant redeployment.

An obvious contribution to police crisis intervention is the movement personified by Carl Rogers, who advanced the notion that key attributes of the counselor (genuineness, accurate empathy, and warmth or unconditional regard) are more important to the process than the professional qualifications or credentials of the counselor (Rogers, 1961). Also of importance is the popularity and success of peer-counseling enterprises such as Alcoholics Anonymous and its derivatives. These ideas and precedents led to the legitimization of the peer-counseling or paraprofessional counseling modality. In policing, the derivation is direct, in that the first peer counselors (introduced in the 1950s) were invoked to deal with problems of alcoholism, and the first crisis intervention activities (debriefings) were Rogerian exercises.

The peer-counseling movement was fortuitously congruent with the traditional police culture, which holds that only an officer can understand another officer and that "you have to have been there to know what it is like." The police culture has also been described as assiduously cultivating social distance from civilians and prizing a measure of cynical realism and a dose of presumably healthy suspiciousness. Moreover, mental health professionals, such as "shrinks," were seen to provide their services to the nonresilient, the defective, and the certifiably insane and certainly not to superbly functioning individuals who happened to have a few routine personal problems.

Finn and Tomz (1997) pointed out that "the training of police officers to provide support to other officers experiencing stress has become a common feature of many law enforcement stress programs" (pp. 56–57). Such training capitalizes on the fact that officers in trouble have been apt to confide in fellow officers to whom they felt close and whom they respected. Finn and Tomz (1997) mentioned the fact that "there have always been a few individuals in every department or post to whom other officers have turned for help in times of crisis" (p. 57). Such "natural" counselors come to the fore because team members are typically chosen through nominations by colleagues and through expressions of interest. Further, "grass-roots expertise" is introduced where team members (such as former alcoholics, officers who have lost a loved one, or officers involved in a shooting in the past) are invoked as products of the problem they are addressing.

Teams typically select their own leaders (coordinators), and these leaders consequently tend to have considerable locker-room credibility. Credibility is the coinage of the peer support process. Finn and Tomz (1997) indicated, for example, that "officers who have used their weapons often feel that no one can understand their turmoil except another officer who has had a similar experience." Such officers feel especially vulnerable (hence, reluctant to talk with nonpeers), because beyond their traumatic shooting experience they feel "disturbed by their department's lack of support in these crisis situations because they are typically relieved of their weapons, interrogated, and subjected to internal department investigation as well as sometimes to a civil suit by the person they shot" (p. 61).

Credibility allows peer support teams to serve "bridging" functions, such as referrals to professional assistance where it is called for. Finn and Tomz (1997) confirmed that "when a referral comes from a trusted peer, many officers are more likely to take advantage of counseling services than if they have to make an appointment on their own or follow the suggestion of a family member or program clinician" (p. 57).

Critical-incident peer support programs are, of course, not a panacea. Nor are they devoid of implementation problems. Some officers prefer to seek help from professionals who presumptively have "real" expertise, and occasionally team members lack the Rogerian attributes their mission requires. They may be unable, for example, to make the transition from detective-type interrogatories to demonstrations of warmth and empathy. Practical and administrative problems also arise, such as the fact that "communication between peer supporters and officers is usually not privileged conversation under the law. . . . As a result, courts and police supervisors have the legal right to ask what was said during these interactions" (p. 59).

Implementation Issues

Among the talks at the FBI's 1989 convocation was a presentation, interestingly subtitled "Lessons Learned," in which Nielsen (1990) detailed some events in the life of the Salt Lake City Police Department's peer support program, the Traumatic Incident Corps (TIC). This team-structured program was established after research had been conducted that showed that officers involved in shootings "preferred to talk with other officers about the experience, but that frequently other officers proved to be a significant source of stress and aggravation" (p. 315).

One of the first discoveries after the establishment of the program was that the team's chain of command tended not to be notified when incidents occurred, so that the team members had to rely on the department's rumor chain to find the officers involved. Having thus learned of occasions in which their presence might be in order, team members "showed personal initiative by interjecting themselves into the situation" (p. 316). The embarrassing problem had to be addressed in standard bureaucratic fashion via a general order that mandated team notification and institutionalized the involvement of team members.

Logistically, it proved advantageous to have the team

made up of patrol officers, ensuring that members were always out on active patrol and could be dispatched to incidents as soon as they took place. The officers operated under the auspices of the psychological services unit and this defined their concern as "the well-being of the individual officer" (p. 317).

Concern with the well-being of the officer, however, proved problematic when that officer was subject to sanction, including criminal charges. In such situations,

> the TIC members have assiduously avoided becoming a conduit of information from the administration to the individual officer. They have, however, worked to arrange resources to assist individual officers that sometimes include the resources of the police department and the police union. (p. 317)

For example, TIC members worked with a suspended officer and his young children to provide financial assistance, including part-time employment for the officer (who was eventually acquitted).[2]

Some problems had to do with impediments to a peer–therapeutic alliance. Nielsen (1990) reported, for example, that

> On at least one occasion since the team came into operation, an officer who was involved in a shooting incident was largely regarded within the department as an inadequate officer who was socially without any relationships. In fact, every member of the team reported no favorable experience with the officer. Ultimately, the peer counselor selected was the person who had had the least to do with the officer, anticipating that under these cir-

---

[2]The stress produced by involvement in a shooting incident can frequently be compounded by the stress engendered by the investigation of the incident. Record (1997) noted that some police departments make their investigatory procedures unnecessarily stressful by providing the officer with no information about what he or she can expect, leading to confusion and fear of the unknown.

cumstances there was less past negative history which would have to be overcome to be of some assistance to the officer. This incident, however, points out that there are probably individuals in every police agency who are largely socially isolated and/or have personalities that do not engender positive reactions on the part of their fellow officers. When these officers become involved in a traumatic incident, it becomes a very difficult task to find someone who has the ability to relate to this individual in an accepting fashion. (p. 318)

Other problems came to the fore when team members were brought in to assist police departments in the vicinity of Salt Lake City. The chiefs of small departments sometimes lacked the fullest appreciation of confidentiality provisions and asked to be kept abreast of team activities. Team members were also sometimes asked to perform functions as broad-gauged therapists or social workers. For example,

In one incident in a rural part of Utah, a small sheriff's office had an incident wherein one deputy sheriff accidentally shot and killed another deputy. Although initial peer support was offered to the involved officer and other members of the agency, the family of the slain officer began to see the peer counselors as potential family therapists. Unfortunately, the family was fraught with a good deal of pathology, and it was necessary to extricate the peer counselors from the situation and refer the family to local mental health resources. (p. 319)

On a similar occasion (again involving an officer killed by a second officer in an accident), the team and its psychologists were asked to assist en masse because "the incident touched virtually everyone employed in the department." Nielsen (1990) reported that "what followed was a chaotic and rushed set of experiences in which the department endeavored to find uses for this large number of peer counselors" (p. 319). This experience underlined the need for attention to the planning of interventions.

The Salt Lake City team expanded its membership to officers with experience in a wide range of traumatic events, so as not to become a "shooters club" of officers who had fired their weapons in a crisis and not to restrict its repertoire and expertise. By the same token, team membership became prestigious, and the assignment became attractive for the wrong reasons, creating a need to weed out aspiring career-ists. The latter were typically characterized by the lack of the attributes prescribed by Rogers for effective counselors. According to Nielsen (1990),

> During training sessions when specific examples are used, this group of officers often become concerned about the "rightness" of the shooting or about the potential of becoming a witness in a civil suit. Experience has shown that when this is the case, these officers typically lack empathy or are largely indifferent to the emotional state of fellow officers and tend to become preoccupied in the technical aspects of the police situation, i.e., conditions for the use of force and/or police tactics, etc. Obviously, people with this type of orientation will be largely ineffective in a peer counseling role and this has been borne out through subsequent events. (p. 320)

Lessons of the kind learned in Salt Lake City have to be re-learned in other jurisdictions that initiate peer support programs for participants in critical incidents. But other lessons may have to be newly learned that vary from one program to the next, depending on organizational attributes, selection and training of team members, types of clients, and incidents to which teams respond. One important issue mentioned by Nielsen (1990) in his review, however, is universally applicable, and this has to do with the prevalence, or dearth, of critical incidents.

Peer support is characterized by high levels of idealism and dedication among participants, a highly developed sense of mission, and esprit de corps. Team members graduate from training experiences eager for the opportunity to apply what they have learned and anxious to assist colleagues in distress who could benefit from their ministrations. What is therefore required by peer counselors are colleagues in distress. But critical incidents occur infrequently in most police departments, and team motivation and skill level may be hard to sustain. Nielsen (1990) suggested periodic meetings and training sessions. Training is, however, best conducted around actual experiences of team members and can be academic (in a pejorative sense) in the absence of such experience. This suggests that before peer support programs are instituted, studies ought to be conducted to confirm that critical incidents of the type to which the teams are to respond occur in appreciable numbers. Although peer support teams are an incredibly exciting innovation, they can become less exciting where few or limited opportunities exist for the deployment of peer support.

Critical-Incident Stress Teams

Although police think of themselves as a unique profession, there are many commonalities in the occupational world when it comes to sources of stress. Corrections officers and police officers, for example, can be bracketed as facing danger on the job, and there are individuals who spend their time guarding prisoners one day and patrolling the streets the next. Where the pressures of shift work are highlighted as contributing to family problems, all sorts of occupational groups lay claim to commensurate concern.

The same holds for critical incidents. Police can be devastated by the death of a colleague, but so can members of other occupations. Miners die trapped in mining accidents, and firefighters die trapped in buildings. A firefighter's funeral has the same pathos and ceremonial quality as that of a police officer who has been shot by an offender. Police officers may be exposed to death or the injury of small children, but so are members of other occupations. When police officers respond to a traumatizing incident, so do ambulance attendants and medical workers. Irrespective of uniform, all must deal with the same shock and sense of helplessness that is engendered by these incidents.

The fact that commonalities exist has led to the broadening of the peer-counseling modality. As pointed out by Jeffrey Mitchell (1990), "law enforcement agencies are joining with their counterparts in fire and emergency medical services to develop multi-agency critical incident teams" (p. 289). Mitchell credited the development to experiences shared by respondents to "such horrific events as airplane crashes, tornadoes, floods and large fires." Through conjoint experiences, "police frequently learned that there was something very positive to be said for immediate support from teams of specially trained mental health professionals and peer support personnel" (p. 290).

Mitchell (1990) discussed police resistance to the broadening of the stress team modality, based on the premise that "no other experience compares to law enforcement." He pointed out, however, that

> disasters and other major events such as line of duty deaths, serious injuries to emergency workers and very traumatic deaths to children tend to strip away the usual defenses and equalize emergency service providers. What remains then is a realization that they are all very much the same regardless of the uniforms or the equipment. They are human beings first and they are vulnerable to being hurt by their jobs. (p. 291)

Once the concept of critical-incident peer support is broadened, different types of team configurations are possible. Mitchell is identified with one such model, which includes a "mixed cadre of peers" as well as mental health professionals. Mitchell also has emphasized the use of "pre-incident stress preparation," although it is not clear how this preparation applies to the typical incident, whose advent cannot be anticipated.

The concept of pre-incident stress preparation is congruent with the prevailing cognitive emphasis in police stress programming, which usually involves didactic approaches such as "stress inoculation." Those who offer such programs assume that factual knowledge (however briefly and passively acquired) can lead to effective coping. Mitchell (1990) himself contended that with preparatory training, "personnel involved in distressing situations generally are better able to avoid stress reactions or they are able to better control their reactions should they occur" (p. 292).

Every police recruit academy currently offers a segment of stress-related lectures. Other stress-related content is provided to most officers in in-service training modules. Sometimes psychologists give such lectures, but they are usually delivered by training academy staff. Where critical-incident teams exist, however, team members can be invoked to provide the training. Aside from the impact, if any, of stress lectures on the trainees, the involvement furnishes a professional development opportunity to team members, although the value of the experience varies depending on the degree to which the training content has been prestructured or prepackaged.

All prepackaging serves to stifle innovation, but new modalities invite the use of standardized materials and detailed prescriptions because this enables programs to be easily introduced and implemented. Prestructuring also assures participants that what they do has been validated and that it is being done elsewhere. Moreover, a modality that takes the same form in many jurisdictions lends itself to networking and collegiality, which are socially reinforcing. When one is doing something that is brave and new, one feels unsure of oneself unless one knows of others who are engaged in the same enterprise elsewhere. Given these advantages, it is hard to appreciate the more subtle rewards of innovation and experimentation.

Structure

The Critical Incident Stress Management (CISM) model prescribed by Mitchell is disseminated by the International Critical Incident Stress Foundation (ICISF). This group offers many kinds of training programs and courses relating to the model that it advocates. With respect to debriefing, for instance, the foundation's instruction covers "a specific seven-phase model which has (1) an introductory phase, (2) a fact phase, (3) a thought phase, (4) a reaction phase, (5) a symptom phase, (6) a teaching/information phase, and (7) a reentry phrase" (Mitchell & Everly, in press, p. 7).

The ICISF claims more than 3,000 members. Those joining the movement are assured that "since 1983, approximately 20,000 'Mitchell model' debriefings have been conducted by almost 400 trained CISM teams through 12 nations" (Robinson & Mitchell, 1995, p. 6). Handouts disseminated by the foundation point out to prospective members that

> The International Critical Incident Stress Foundation, Inc., [ICISF] has trained and has members in the Federal Bureau of Investigation, the United States Marshals Service, the United States Secret Service, the United States Drug Enforcement Agency, the Central Intelligence Agency, all branches of the United States military, the United Nations, the Royal Canadian Mounted Police, the Swedish National Police, FEMA [(U.S.) Federal Emergency Management Agency], Social Development Office —State of Kuwait, and the Red Cross.
>
> ICISF has teams in all fifty United States, Guam and sixteen foreign nations, including: Australia, Canada, Finland, Germany, Great Britain, Iceland, Japan, Kuwait, New Zealand, Northern Ireland, Norway, Peru, South Africa, Spain, Sweden, and Switzerland. Teams represent the various fire, police, emergency medical services, and rescue companies within these areas.
>
> ICISF has also trained members of AirBC, the Airline Pilots Association, Continental Airlines, General Motors, the Seventh Day Adventists, United Airlines, United Auto Workers, USAir, and World Airways.

Teams as Organizational Innovations

The Madison Avenue approach to marketing team training and consultation raises questions about the modality as an organizational intervention. These questions are important because teams offer exciting possibilities for police reform. As is true of other specialty areas (see chapter 7), stress reduction is an activity that centers on a problem (is problem oriented) and applies knowledge to the solution of the problem. The fact that the stress-reducing activity is performed by teams matters a great deal, because teams engage in group problem solving collaboratively. Teams also lend themselves to union–management sponsorship and (as we have seen) to interagency cooperation.

Stress reduction teams combine individual-change and organizational-change features. The fact that team members are people who have experienced a problem and can thereby assist others who face the problem makes this type of counseling a powerful individual-change modality. The fact that most teams are made up of peer-nominated members and that they elect their coordinators makes them uniquely able to tackle cultural norms that are ordinarily impervious to intervention. Stress teams thus have credibility in the locker room despite "social work" connotations and the fact that teams deal in commodities such as vulnerability and compassion and promote the surfacing and expression of self-doubt, fear, and existential angst.

Where teams gain experience, they are uniquely able to build knowledge by analyzing the successes and failures of their interventions. This process is individual in that team members perfect their expertise and enhance their professional stature. It is organizational because teams contribute what they learn to their organization and to other teams, who are in a position to reciprocate. What can thus result is a field of knowledge that is cumulatively enriched by collective experience and systematic review.

For teams to build knowledge, they must recognize it when they acquire it. Teams are unlikely to learn from their experience if they underestimate its value. They cannot assume that what is worth knowing has been discovered by experts and disseminated through training. They cannot assume that what they have to do is simply to apply available prescriptions.

The very worst that can happen to stress reduction teams is for the movement to become institutionalized, ritualized, and ossified. Teams must be engaged, if need be by expanding their purview and jurisdiction. They must function as teams, plan activities, and review and digest experiences. They must relate to their organization and other organizations, to ensure their responsiveness to needs. They must network with those who are similarly engaged, to compare and systematize experiences.

Most important, team members as human beings must retain the qualities of genuineness, accurate empathy, and warmth that Carl Rogers prescribed. And those qualities are lost, Rogers has often warned us, by bureaucrats and jaded professionals. Those who help in mechanistic fashion, by just "doing a job" or merely following prescribed routines, are perceived by their clients as cold and uncaring. Instead of reducing stress, such people are apt to preserve and even to increase it.

Critical-Incident Study Teams

Team activities can be enhanced by expanding the range of critical incidents to which the teams respond. Involvement can also be enhanced by broadening the mission of teams beyond that of assisting officers to cope with stress in crises.

One of the most innovative suggestions for an expanded team mission is by policing expert James Fyfe, who has pointed out that "peer group members can be used to help define the appropriate ways to deal with potentially violent and tragic situations and to turn them into highly credible training" (J. J. Fyfe, personal communication, 2001, February 3). For Fyfe, the study of critical incidents by team members can yield substantive knowledge that can be shared through training. Such knowledge can assist officers to improve their assessment and handling of critical situations. Instead of a focus on stress inoculation, this model centers on incident inoculation, on the assumption that any situations that are more effectively dealt with are less likely to produce stress.

According to Fyfe,

A big part of the stress of policing is the ambiguity that

accompanies so much of it. Officers are given only rudimentary guidance and introduction in, e.g., how to stop a car containing a felony suspect; how to deal with the emotionally disturbed; how to respond to a robbery; how to deal with hostage and barricade situations; when and how much to pursue. The consequence is that they play these things by ear in the most trying and urgent circumstances, and that they often make mistakes they have to live with. Thus, a good part of stress training should be designed to transmit competencies so that police can: be assured that they know the best professional thinking about how to solve the most vexing and dangerous police situations. This is a confidence builder that reduces anticipating stress.

☐ know that, even if situations have ended badly, they have done what they were supposed to do.
☐ know that their performance will be evaluated on the basis of what they did, rather than on the basis of outcomes that often are accidental and beyond the control of the police.

Evaluation of performance is important because much of police officers' critical-incident stress is attributed to the experience of being second-guessed when their interventions misfire. Fyfe pointed out that by contrast, "in all real professions (medicine, law), performance is judged on process rather than outcome." Officers who are taught to be mindfully involved in assessing crisis situations to which they have to respond can gain confidence and achieve competence, which can buy immunity from ex-post-facto condemnation.

Fyfe (1986) has asserted that police must first and foremost be skilled "diagnosticians." Critical-incident study teams can become a credible vehicle for enhancing the diagnostic acumen of fellow officers and the effectiveness of their responses to difficult situations. The goal of the process would be stress reduction through enhanced competence via peer intervention.

9

Retrospect

It is axiomatic that the most scintillating scientific inquiries are those in which one's hypotheses are disconfirmed. Because our expectations were scant and tentative, we had a great deal to learn. In this chapter I detail what I think we have learned from our explorations.

Politics

At the inception of this report, I suggested that our principal goal was to examine the relationship between stress and police reform. By this I had in mind contemporary, ongoing developments, such as community-oriented policing and diversification of the police force.

An emendation is now in order. Shortly after the inception of our project, it became clear to us that in both police departments, the hands-down winner of the Red-Flag Stressor Award was the concept of "politics." In a more restricted sense, politics in the city department had to do with administrative discretion in promotions to the detective division. But there was a great deal of baggage to the term, relating to favoritism, cronyism, discrimination, ingrouping, outgrouping, inequity, injustice, arbitrariness, lack of quality control, rewards for incompetence, and failure to recognize achievement.

A number of diverse findings proved related to each other: In self-anchoring scales, the officers defined their ideal police department as a professionally proficient meritocracy; their least admired department was judged sloppy and unfair. In focus groups and in the survey itself, concerns about managerial arbitrariness evoked bitterness and resentment. When we discussed survey results, the suggestions made by officers revolved around rewards for demonstrations of competence.

These facts are related. Although police officers' resentments of administrative practices have emerged in other studies, the resentments have not generally been tied to the notion that quality performance is compromised by endemic arbitrariness. Among officers, this notion was strongly held and almost obsessive.

Reasons for strong feelings may be partly contemporary and partly historical. The history plausibly has to do with past efforts at reform and their sediments, because any reform strategy presents a distinct set of problems for targets of reform and embodies a distinct set of stressors.

Typically, American police agencies at the turn of the last century grappled with the realities of political interference in departmental operations (Walker, 1992). During this period, municipal governments were shaped by party "machines," which operated a spoils system in which faithful acolytes were rewarded with appointments and promotions to positions in city government. The system was in fact extremely arbitrary, in that "who you knew" (who owed you personal loyalty) mattered more than "what you knew" (your competence and integrity). Municipal services—including policing—were thus lax or inefficient and redolent with corruption.

In metropolitan police departments, the reaction to this state of affairs took the form of what has been called "reform policing," which highlighted centralized, bureaucratic organizations, with a top-down management and a no-holds-barred, full-enforcement philosophy. One downside of these otherwise meritorious developments was a set of stressors for the officers and a related one for citizens. The officers had to cope with rigid, heavy-handed managerial practices and command-and-control administrations. The citizens were in turn subjected to inflexible, impersonal policing and often saw the police as an occupying force patrolling conquered terrain.

Again in partial reaction, a new set of reforms was instituted, culminating in currently prevailing philosophies of community-oriented and problem-oriented policing. These new reforms have offended a new set of targets of reform— those employees most strongly wedded to preceding orientations and practices.

Not all municipalities in the country proceeded through this standard sequence at an equivalent pace. In some cities, the 19th-century party machine approach to local politics and government survived well into the 20th century.[1] Where this occurred—as it very much did in the setting in which our study took place—a truncated historical experience substituted for the fully developed police reform model with its stable bureaucratic structure. Among the attributes of this experience were (a) successive departmental administrations that varied quite sharply in philosophies and practices, (b) acrimonious labor negotiations producing agreements that emphasized punctilious adherence to formalistic rules, and (c) endemic sensitivity to managerial practices perceived to be survivals of the pre-reform political system.

The psychological salience of machine politics in the minds of officers is pronounced in our city department, where external politics and internal politics were equivalent objects of concern. Machine politics has traditionally been less of a feature of suburban government in the United States.

The fact that the political past remains alive for city officers may partly reflect the actual persistence of anachronistic practices. The disproportionateness of feelings, however, sug-

---

[1]Guyot (1991) described in detail a sequence of this kind affecting the operations of a municipal police department.

gests undigested trauma, collective posttraumatic stress as a pathological organizational syndrome.

Middle-Age and Seniority

Among individual-level attributes, the age of officers was prominently related to level of reported stress. Older officers said they were more stressed than did younger officers. The correlation was substantial, and it was sufficiently strong to cancel increments in stress among female and non-White officers, all of whom were young and had little seniority. To study differences in experienced stress between equivalent male and female officers and among comparable officers of different ethnic backgrounds, time must elapse for seniority to cumulate. And, once this occurs, differences are likely to emerge. Indications that this is so include the perception by female and non-White officers that they are targets of discrimination. There is also evidence that the acceptance of female officers by male officers is not yet universally unqualified.

Statistically, age and seniority are a single variable; conceptualiy, they are separable. Sometimes age itself is at issue, and sometimes it is seniority. Family stress is largely related to age. As workers get older, their families age as well: The middle-aged person can become "sandwiched" between maturing offspring and dependent parents—frequently under one roof. Adult children leave home and fail or rebel, finances become strained, and marriages painfully dissolve. All career stages have their problems, but some stages have more problems than others.

Seniority is chiefly at issue in work-related stress. Cumulative exposure to client problems can lead to burnout (Cherniss, 1980), although this appears not to be much a factor in policing. Slower-than-hoped-for advancement and less-than-anticipated recognition can become sources of frustration. Probably most to the point, given the history of our police departments, is exposure to turbulent work environments over time, which becomes the occasion for discomfort.

With approaching retirement, one also expects stress to increase, because career changes are no longer a viable option.

Personal and Organizational Problems

Sources and consequences of stress are not neatly separable. Family problems affect work performance, and job-related problems contaminate family life. Problems can also cumulate, so that stress responses are hard to attribute to one source or another. Moreover, coping (or rather, noncoping) with any stressor can invite additional problems, producing chain reactions of compounded or accelerating stress.

Some modal patterns do appear for officers under stress. One such pattern is purely organization related. It has to do with alienation and disengagement. Our officers hypothesized such a pattern when they asked, "Do you think that your level of motivation or commitment has been diminished by any actions of the Department's administration?" Affirmative responses to such questions postulate decrements in work motivation attributable to inadequate recognition of performance or inequitable opportunity systems.

A modal pattern that is person centered had to do with experiences involving death, injury, and suffering—especially involving children. Experiences of this kind were not seen to produce decrements in performance at work or emotional disengagement (burnout). Instead, they were seen to affect dealings with members of officers' families or to lead to excess alcohol consumption. Such experiences were also of concern in relation to what officers talk about with significant others, including spouses and peers.

Person-centered stress is traditionally addressed with person-centered interventions. These programs provide or broker counseling services. Group or individual counseling has also been deployed to help officers to digest traumatic experiences, such as involvements in shootings or exposure to human tragedy. Counseling has been seen as a way to assist officers to resolve interpersonal problems, at home or at work. Family therapy may become possible when the various participants in the evolving conflicts agree to be counseled.

Person-centered interventions can also be invoked in addressing stress-related dysfunctional behavior. Alcohol abuse is, unsurprisingly, the mainstay of employee assistance programs; situational or clinical depression (which can become a prelude to suicide) is a priority concern. Referral of officers to supportive services, such as help with child care or emergency financial assistance, may be considered among expanded employee assistance activities.

Among resistances to person-centered interventions are client concerns about confidentiality and about the ability of the counselor to relate to the experiences of police. The latter concern leads to a demand for peer counseling as a modality. I have reviewed this approach in its original manifestation. A variant that was nominated by the officers we interviewed (see chapter 6) was that of having police officers trained and credentialed to do professional counseling. Psychologists with police backgrounds have already functioned as clinicians in police departments (Reese, 1987). Such people may additionally be deployable as internal consultants.

Organization-related stress—which is the principal problem that officers claim—would appear to call for organization-related interventions. In 1985, Gary Kaufman, who is in charge of psychological services at the Michigan State Police, explained to an American Psychological Association audience that "the emphasis placed upon person-targeted programs by psychologists and police administrators has overshadowed the importance of addressing organizational stressors affecting the line officer" (p. 10). In making this assertion, Kaufman was not talking himself out of a job or biting the hand that employs him. He was, in fact, offering to enrich and enhance the contribution of psychologists to policing.

Kaufman's point was that stress intervention must be multimodal and that this is not a zero-sum game. We can thus "inoculate" recruits to the stressors they may encounter, but we can also reduce the chances that they will encounter them. We could in fact start by treating the recruits as adults in the training academy, instead of self-consciously deploying de-meaning regimentation and calling this a desirable "stress training" model. We can work with individually distressed officers and conjointly remedy the occasions for distress.

Accomplishing one task without the other is insufficient. The mid-career officers described in chapter 4 are ill served if we teach them to do physical exercises and to practice re-laxation techniques, provide them with some marital coun-seling, and let them resign with disability pay or re-expose them to frustrations. We need to draw lessons from their sit-uations and from the cumulative—and by now univocal—literature on occupational stress.

We know a great deal today about how we can promote congruence between organizational environments and hu-man needs. We need to deploy this knowledge or ask why we are not doing so. The query is posed by Terry (1981), who wrote that "organizational reform . . . seems to have taken a back seat to other alternatives, even though there is consid-erable evidence from the organizational literature that more participatory styles of organization and leadership produce greater work satisfaction" (p. 72).

Zhao, Thuman, and He (1999) have similarly pointed out that "the importance of the work environment, particularly autonomy and feedback, is consistent with the premise of the behavioral school of management theory" and that "research has shown that police officers like to work in an environment where they enjoy considerable freedom to decide what they will do" (p. 168). The challenge is to think of ways of en-hancing rank-and-file participation in the administration of police departments. Reiser (1974) wrote more than 20 years ago that

> More enlightened police leadership is aware that man-agement by participation is necessary in order to move from the stifling effect of the pecking order to the ener-getic involvement and commitment of employees who are actively identified with management. These admin-istrators recognize that . . . without the interest and con-scientious enthusiasm of the individuals comprising it,

> the organization can only limp along ineffectually, fighting both internal and external battles. In implementing participative management concepts, modern police managers are utilizing approaches such as decentralized team policing, territorial responsibility, and an open system between policemen, the press, and the community. (p. 157)

There are trends today that augue favorably for organizational reforms. One such trend—which is cited in chapter 7—is that of problem-oriented policing, because this can include problem-oriented approaches to the solution of problems *within* the organization (Toch & Grant, 1981). Problem-oriented approaches are in fact taken in managing police departments, although they fly variegated flags, depending on fashions of the time. Police agencies have fielded task forces, teams, quality of work life groups, and quality circles. Current nomenclature favors the appellation "total quality management" (TQM), although only one police department (Couper & Lobitz, 1991; Wycoff & Skogan, 1993) has approximated the original TQM prescription (Deming, 1986), which requires an organization-wide reform.

Common denominators obscured by language are combinations of (a) groups that represent different specialties and ranks (including rank-and-file officers), which are assigned to study problems and to suggest solutions; (b) the use of data in studying problems; (c) the participation of police unions in the process; and (d) the use of teams—primarily composed of rank-and-file officers—to implement solutions to problems. The model is participatory and excludes a variety of other approaches, such as assigning managers or specialists to come up with data-based solutions to organizational problems. Because stress in policing results from top-down managerial practices, it obviously cannot be ameliorated through undiluted top-down organizational solutions.

As previously noted (see chapter 8), interventions that are designed to ameliorate critical-incident-related stress tend to be participatory in nature and qualify as organizational reforms. One of the elements in such interventions is the deployment of teams and the mobilization of supportive peer interactions. The interventions have also highlighted the importance of union involvement. Finn and Tomz (1997) pointed out that

> The union or association can be a particularly important element in the success of a stress program. For example, in some jurisdictions unions have stymied any peer support program by demanding that officers be paid overtime or given compensatory time whenever they provide peer support; in others they have jeopardized the entire program by telling members that the counselors . . . are a tool of management. Conversely, a union can promote the program to its members and their spouses, refer officers who need assistance (who often call union officials on matters related to drinking or suicide), arrange in some cases for the use of program services in conjunction with or in place of disciplinary measures, and either provide resources itself for the program or influence the department to invest money or staff in it. (p. 93)

A special dilemma in organizational reform is posed by the perception that administrators' decisions are arbitrary or politically tainted. Managers can respond to this perception by instituting a rigid, bureaucratic system that circumscribes decisions and invites litigation about the applications of rules to individual cases. Instead of defusing complaints and ameliorating resentments, this system can increase polarization and the acrimoniousness of union–management disputes. Although the solution is arguably preferable to the problem, it presents a clear need for modifications in the formula. The challenge is to somehow restore trust and allow for collaborative decision making. One must provide for exceptions to rules (such as the consideration of special qualifications of officers for some assignments that are otherwise covered by seniority provisions) to produce sensible outcomes that serve the interests of both the organization and the individual whose career is at issue. A system that prevents efficacious and humane decisions because they "may set a precedent" is an instrument that cuts off one's nose to spite one's face.

For example, if we agree that officers in charge of training must be chosen with exquisite care, we cannot set up a training officer program by insisting on punctilious adherence to seniority rules. If as a result of such a system we have no training officer program at all, we have an example of a non-solution to a problem.

Diverging Perceptions

The most obdurate situation highlighted in our stress study is that of race relations, which, on the face of it, appears to defy easy resolution. The problem illustrates the role of perception in the genesis of stress, because officers subscribe to mutually exclusive versions of its causes.

It is possible for one group of officers to be favored in one area and discriminated against in another, but such is not the contention of the officers in our study. Disparities in perception occur in which each party believes that the other receives preferential treatment in personnel and disciplinary dispositions. Each party believes that it is shortchanged in the allocation of rewards and is disproportionately penalized for transgressions.

It is not immediately obvious how such perceptions about equity and fairness can ever be reconciled. Different versions of unfairness often rest on divergent interpretations of publicly known facts. The same facts lead to the annunciated conclusion that minority officers are disproportionately penalized and to complaints that infractions committed by minority officers are regularly overlooked. Identical facts about promotions and assignments undergird the accusation that White men are favored and that they are shortchanged by affirmative action decisions. Inferences that are drawn from the same data disquietingly lead to diametrically opposite conclusions. On the face of it, it is therefore unlikely that disclosures of additional information are liable to solve this problem. As a case in point, after officers were told at our research site that the assignment of detectives had been systematized, the decibel-level of their complaints about the tainted nature of the process was unaffected. The officers would listen politely to the announcement that a promotional examination had been instituted but would then appear to ignore the news.

Our advisory group had listed communication as an area of concern. The same heading was also highlighted in feedback sessions. But to our officers, "communication" meant "lack of communication." This concept includes withholding vital job-related information and thereby endangering an officer's life. Officers said that they felt that they are routinely kept in the dark about every subject of concern to them. To the officers, this is an issue not only of who is not routing which documents to whom, but also of who is hoarding the data to prevent them from doing their job. The picture conveyed is of an organization working at cross-purposes with itself or of members of the organization working at cross-purposes with each other. In that sense, "communication" comes to mean conflicts, or the perception of conflicts. In Kirschman's (1997) composite police department, for example,

> The detective bureau is unhappy with how patrol officers write reports, and patrol officers think the detectives hoard information. . . . The cops are angry with the way communicators dispatch calls for service at the same time the communicators can't stand the cops for not answering up. Two communicators can't stand working the same shift together. The front desk people are angry with the data-entry folks. Clerks are frustrated because the cops don't check the right boxes on their reports. The detectives are angry because the D.A. won't file on a perfectly good case. The D.A. is angry because the case report is sloppy and weak. . . . The chief is angry at being misquoted by the media, and everyone is angry with the chief. (pp. 52–53)

This is not conflict that arises because one has experienced lapses of communication; it is conflict one sees as having produced these lapses. To end up believing the former can be a significant advance over believing the latter, because it permits questions about improving the flow of information.

It is conceivable that de-escalation of the same sort could ameliorate problems between White and ethnic minority officers because these are premised on assumptions about bad faith by the other party. Officers appear to converge on the value of professional conduct and the importance of high-quality work. Each group, however, assumes that the other is willing to compromise or subvert such goals. This assumption frames the question about whether Gerald Jones merited his promotion or whether Joan Ipswich was disproportionately penalized. And because the administration makes personnel decisions, each group sees the administration as siding with the other group. The administration can therefore be seen as compromising quality productivity, which is a goal it ostensibly strives for.

It is remotely possible that some softening of positions might occur if data were collected and analyzed by the officers themselves. The suggestion (see chapter 6) that officers be rotated through the unit that dispenses disciplinary sanctions (internal affairs) is an example of active involvement in data collection. A similar experiential strategy might be applicable to promotional decisions.

Racial relations are not defined as an intergroup problem but as an organizational one, although officers sometimes allude to individual acts of discrimination. Gender relations, however, are defined as a matter of individual attitudes, of doubts raised by male officers about the competence of female officers. There are also issues relating to insensitivity, chauvinism, and innuendo or of personal conflicts. Problems such as these may be subjects of complaints, but they do not increase occupational stress, as do problems of ethnic relations. Police departments are mostly viewed as gender neutral and moderately dispassionate. Even male extremists (officers who grumble about the proliferation of women) see no "political" bias at work. Women are not seen as inappropriately hired but as personally deficient because they are small, weak, and presumptively timid. By the same token, female officers see chauvinists as patronizing and boorish and not as exemplifying an organizational philosophy.

Gender-related problems are difficult to address for several complicated reasons. For one, the male prejudices that are at issue are tied into traditional macho conceptions of police work that are subculturally respectable, although they are in fact arguably anachronistic. Some women are understandably reluctant to challenge these sorts of assumptions, and many women indicate that they have bought into that perspective. Alissa Worden (1993), who studied the attitudes of men and women officers, reported that

> findings offer little support for the thesis that female officers define their role or see their clientele differently than do males. . . . These findings are also consistent with other studies of police and correctional officers that find few differences in role definition, attitudes toward civilians, and job satisfaction between men and women. (p. 229)

Female officers also do not tend to form or join groups that represent gender-related interests, and they view gender-related problems that they encounter as interpersonal. This fact suggests that the best vehicle for addressing these problems may be to encourage women who are subjected to offensive behavior to seek redress through a designated unit established for that purpose. The unit could then compile complaints to establish patterns of discriminatory conduct.

A Methodological Caveat

I have reported some data that are at best suggestive. Interpretations of the city survey calls for particular caution, because the return rate for this survey was low. On the plus side, our findings appear to converge with those reported by other students of policing.

There are admittedly gaps in our review of stress-related problems. For example, we have not covered the issue of facing danger on the job. Police officers do not customarily raise the subject of fear, and we failed to specifically include it in our inquiry. Only one officer broached the matter spontaneously, and his comment is testimony to what we might have discovered through survey or interview questions. The officer relayed an incident that had to do with his undercover narcotics work:

> Everybody around there got guns, and you introduce yourself, and he will give you his name. He gives you whatever name in Spanish, and he looks at you and he says my name means, I Fear no Death. What am I here for? What am I here for? I am dealing with a man that just gave me his name and looked me in the face and said his name means he fears no death . . . I am already thinking, okay now, what am I gonna do? If this thing goes sour and my backup team is three blocks away. Three blocks away does not give you comfort. You are by yourself with maybe an informant, and he is shaky as it is. That is why he is an informant. You already know he's a snake. You don't become an informant unless you're a snake, right?
> . . . He ain't going to protect me. I got to protect myself. . . . Now I got to convince you [I am] who you think that I'm not. Cause you're already wondering if I am a cop. So I got to convince you that I'm not. I got to convince you that I am a hustler. That I am only interested in buying the product and selling the product. . . .

Nowadays, "police fear" is openly dealt with in training programs. Several departments—such as the Michigan State Police—have pioneered in defining fear management as a stress-related area. A training manual developed by California Peace Officers (1993) and used by the Michigan State Police noted that

> all law enforcement officers on patrol have experienced fear to some degree. . . . In the past, peace officers viewed fear in other officers as unprofessional and incompetent.

For the first time, the profession is recognizing that it is
natural and human for police to acknowledge fear. (p. 8)

In relation to fear-provoking incidents, the manual suggested
to "talk with peers and professionals 'when safe' regarding
your reactions, thoughts and feelings during the situation"
(p. 15). Working through experiences of fear thus becomes a
mainline task for debriefings.

Contingent Events

Although sponsorship of our study was in many ways ideal,
we feel that the benefits of the self-study process can be further enhanced. Our suburban survey was self-administered
and yielded comprehensive coverage. Conditions in that department were also auspicious for the utilization of findings.
We are less happy with our city involvements, which was
hampered by a change in administration.

There is clearly no way of anticipating unforeseeable developments. One such event was a critical incident—the killing of an officer by an armed suspect during the course of
our study. Such incidents can obviously significantly affect
the results of a study. As noted in chapter 8, many survey
respondents said, "the shooting of an on-duty officer" was
their principal occasion for stress. The capture of the offender
provided some relief or ameliorative satisfaction, and the
shooting created solidarity in the ranks and improved community relations. The experience also suggested to us the
need to attend to critical-incident stress.

Chapter 7 is also the result of a project-related experience.
During a visit to a precinct run by an innovative command-
ing officer who participated in our study, we were introduced
to a team of officers who had developed a unique area of
expertise. The precinct is ethnically heterogeneous. It con-
tains, among other ethnic groups, Arab merchants who operate more than 30 retail stores. When these corner stores
became targets of drug dealers and gang members in search
of sites for drug dealing and fraternal conviviality, two pre-

cinct officers became interested in the store owners. This interest blossomed into intensive research and academic work, with the officers ending up as grassroots experts in Middle Eastern culture and language. A second team of officers in the same precinct originated a successful project on their own involving the repurchase of citizen-owned weapons. Both sets of officers—and their precinct commander—became concerned that the level of recognition accorded to these projects was not commensurate with the level of ingenuity exercised by the officers. The issue thus posed is among those addressed in chapter 7.

Historical developments are not under researcher control, although their results can be studied. We had no way of anticipating some of the project-related developments we encountered. We could not have prevented the trust problems that outsiders such as ourselves must overcome in working with officers. The best one can probably do when such problems arise is to avoid defensiveness and allow participants to exert restorative peer influence. The resignation of our city host (the commissioner who had worked with us on the project) became problematic because his successors had no investment in the study. We were unsuccessful in kindling the requisite enthusiasm. However, our officer–researchers remain in place, and it is possible that they can some day contribute to the enactment of reforms.

References

Alex, N. (1969). *Black in blue: A study of the Negro policeman.* New York: Appleton-Century-Crofts.

Andrews, L. (1996). *Suicide in the RCMP: 1984–1995.* Ottawa, Ontario, Canada: Royal Canadian Mounted Police.

Axelbred, M., & Valle, J. (1978). *Stress control program for police officers: City of Miami Police Department.* Miami, FL: Counseling and Stress Control Center, Miami Police Department.

Baker, J. C. (1999). *Danger, duty and disillusion: The worldview of Los Angeles police officers.* Prospect Heights, IL: Waveland Press.

Belknap, J., & Shelley, J. K. (1992). The new Lone Ranger: Policewomen on patrol. *American Journal of Police, 12*(2), 47–75.

Berg, B. L., & Budnick, K. J. (1986). Defeminization of women in law enforcement: A new twist in the traditional police personality. *Journal of Police Science and Administration, 14,* 314–319.

Blak, R. (1990). Critical incident debriefing for law enforcement personnel. In J. T. Reese, J. M. Horn, & C. Dumming (Eds.), *Critical incidents in policing* (pp. 39–50). Washington, DC: Federal Bureau of Investigation.

Brown, J. M., & Campbell, E. A. (1994). *Stress and policing: Sources and strategies.* Chichester, England: Wiley.

Bureau of Justice Assistance. (1990). *Preventing law enforcement stress: The organization's role.* Washington, DC: Author.

California Peace Officers. (1993). *Training manual: Fear management telecourse.* Lansing: Michigan State Police Behavioral Science Section.

Caplan, G. (1964). *Principles of preventive psychiatry.* New York: Basic Books.

Cherniss, C. (1980). *Professional burnout in human service organizations.* New York: Praeger.

Couper, D. C., & Lobitz, S. H. (1991). *Quality policing: The Madison experience.* Washington, DC: Police Executive Research Forum.

Crank, J. P., & Caldero, M. (1991). The production of occupational stress in medium-sized police agencies: A survey of line officers in eight municipal police departments. *Journal of Criminal Justice, 19,* 339–349.

Dantzer, M. L., & Kubin, B. (1998). Job satisfaction: The gender perspective among police officers. *American Journal of Criminal Justice, 23,* 19–31.

Deming, W. E. (1986). *Out of crisis.* Cambridge, MA: MIT Press.

Elliot, M. L., Bingham, R. D., Nielsen, S. C., & Warner, P. D. (1986). Marital intimacy and satisfaction as a support system for coping with police officer stress. *Journal of Police Science and Administration, 14,* 40–44.

Ellison, K. W., & Genz, J. L. (1978). Police officer as burned-out Samaritan. *FBI Law Enforcement Bulletin, 47,* 2–7.

Ellison, K. W., & Genz, J. L. (1983). *Stress and the police officer.* Springfield, IL: Charles C Thomas.

213

Fennell, J. T. (1981). Psychological stress and the peace officer, or stress—a cop killer. In G. Henderson (Ed.), *Police human relations* (pp. 170–179). Springfield, IL: Charles C Thomas.

Finn, P., & Tomz, J. E. (1997). *Developing a law enforcement stress program for officers and their families*. Washington, DC: National Institute of Justice.

Flynn, K. (2000, December 26). Police feel scorn on beat and pressure from above. *New York Times*, pp. A1, B6.

French, W. L., & Bell, C. H. (1999). *Organization development: Behavioral science interventions for organization improvement* (6th ed.). Englewood Cliffs, NJ: Prentice-Hall.

Fuller, R. A. (1987). An overview of the process of peer support team development. In J. T. Reese, J. M. Horn, & C. Dunning (Eds.), *Critical incidents in policing* (pp. 149–158). Washington, DC: Federal Bureau of Investigation.

Fyfe, J. J. (1986). The split-second syndrome and other determinants of police violence. In A. Campbell & J. J. Gibbs (Eds.), *Violent transactions* (pp. 207–224). Oxford, England: Basil Blackwell.

Gentz, D. (1990). The psychological impact of critical incidents on police officers. In J. T. Reese, J. M. Horn, & C. Dunning (Eds.), *Critical incidents in policing* (pp. 175–181). Washington, DC: Federal Bureau of Investigation.

Gentz, D. (1994). Critical incident reactions. *Journal of Police and Criminal Psychology, 10*, 35–37.

Gold, D. (1990). Adjusting to destiny with grace and dignity. In J. T. Reese, J. M. Horn, & C. Dunning (Eds.), *Critical incidents in policing* (pp. 181–192). Washington, DC: Federal Bureau of Investigation.

Goldstein, H. (1980). *Problem-oriented policing*. New York: McGraw Hill.

Gordon, S. (1980, September/October). Workplace fantasies. *Working Papers for New Society*, pp. 39–41.

Greene, H. T. (1997, March). *An exploratory study of the history of Black women in policing*. A paper presented at the Academy of Criminal Justice Sciences annual meeting, Louisville, KY.

Guyot, D. (1991). *Policing as though people matter*. Philadelphia: Temple University Press.

Haarr, R. N., & Morash, M. (1999). Gender, race, and strategies of coping with occupational stress in policing. *Justice Quarterly, 16*, 303–336.

Hale, D. C., & Wyland, S. M. (1993). Dragons and dinosaurs: The plight of patrol women. *Police Forum, 3*, 1–6.

Herzberg, F., Mausner, B., & Snyderman, B. B. (1959). *The motivation to work*. New York: Wiley.

Herzberg, F., Mausner, B., & Snyderman, B. B. (1993). *The motivation to work*. New Brunswick, NJ: Transaction.

Hochstedler, E., & Conley, J. A. (1986). Explaining underrepresentation of Black officers in city police agencies. *Journal of Criminal Justice, 14*, 319–328.

Holdaway, S., & Barron, A. M. (1997). *Resigners? The experience of Black and Asian police officers.* London: MacMillan.

Kardiner, A., & Spiegel, S. (1947). *War, stress, and neurotic illness.* New York: Hoeber.

Kaufman, G. (1985, August). *Law enforcement organizational health consultation.* Presentation at the meeting of the American Psychological Association, Los Angeles.

Kirschman, E. (1997). *I love a cop: What police families need to know.* New York: Guilford Press.

Kirschman, E., Scrivner, E., Ellison, K., & Mercy, C. (1992). Work and well-being: Lessons from law enforcement. In J. C. Quick, L. R. Murphy, & J. J. Hurell, Jr. (Eds.), *Stress and well-being at work: Assessments and interventions for occupational mental health* (178–192). Washington, DC: American Psychological Association.

Klein, R. (1990). The utilization of police counselors in critical incident stress. In J. T. Reese, J. M. Horn, & C. Dunning (Eds.), *Critical incidents in policing* (pp. 235–248). Washington, DC: Federal Bureau of Investigation.

Lanier, M. M. (1996). An evolutionary typology of women police officers. *Women and Criminal Justice, 8*(2), 35–57.

Lersch, K. L. (1998). Exploring gender differences in citizen allegations of misconduct: An analysis of a municipal police department. *Women and Criminal Justice, 9*(4), 69–79.

Levy, C. J. (1999, March 25). Albany to pass bill to benefit prison guards. *New York Times*, p. B1.

Lewin, K. (1946). Action research and minority problems. *Journal of Social Issues, 2,* 34–46.

Lewin, K. (1947). Group decision and social change. In T. M. Newcomb, E. L. Hartley, & Editorial Committee (Eds.), *Readings in social psychology* (pp. 330–344). New York: Henry Holt.

Lewis, R. (1973). Toward an understanding of police anomie. *Journal of Police Science and Administration, 1,* 484–490.

Lindemann, E. (1944). Symptomatology and management of acute grief. *American Journal of Psychiatry, 101,* 141–148.

MacGregor, D. (1960). *The human side of enterprise.* New York: McGraw-Hill.

Martin, S. E. (1980). *Breaking and entering: Policewomen on patrol.* Berkeley: University of California Press.

Martin, S. E. (1994). An outsider within the station house: The impact of race and gender on Black women police. *Social Problems, 41,* 383–400.

Maslow, A. H. (1970). *Motivation and personality.* New York: Harper.

Mitchell, J. T. (1990). Law enforcement applications of critical incident stress teams. In J. T. Reese, J. M. Horn, & C. Dunning (Eds.), *Critical incidents in policing* (pp. 289–302). Washington, DC: Federal Bureau of Investigation.

Mitchell, J. T., & Everly, G. S. (in press). Critical incident stress management and critical incident stress debriefings: Evolutions, effects, and outcomes. In B. Raphael & J. Wilson (Eds.), *Psychological debriefing*. London: Oxford.

Molloy, T. E., & Mays, G. L. (1984). The police stress hypothesis: A critical evaluation. *Criminal Justice and Behavior, 11*, 197–229.

Morash, M., & Haarr, R. N. (1995). Gender, workplace problems, and stress in policing. *Justice Quarterly, 12*, 113–140.

National Institute of Justice. (1999). At a glance: Recent research findings. *National Institute of Justice Journal, 27*.

New York State United Teachers. (1981, December 20). Stress/burnout study sheds new light on issues involved. *New York Teacher*, p. 10.

Nielsen, E. (1990). Traumatic Incident Corps: Lessons learned. In J. T. Reese, J. M. Horn, & C. Dunning (Eds.), *Critical incidents in policing* (pp. 315–323). Washington, DC: Federal Bureau of Investigation.

On-the-job-stress in policing: Reducing it, preventing it. (2000, January). *National Institute of Justice Journal*, 18–24.

Pugh, G. M. (1986). The good police officer: Qualities, roles, and concepts. *Journal of Police Science and Administration, 14*, 1–5.

Reaves, B. A. (1996a). *Law enforcement management and administrative statistics, 1993: Data for individual state and local agencies with 100 or more officers*. Washington, DC: Bureau of Justice Statistics.

Reaves, B. A. (1996b). *Local police departments, 1993*. Washington, DC: U.S. Department of Justice.

Record, N. (1997). Surviving the stress of officer-involved shootings. *Sheriff, 49*, 12–14.

Reese, J. T. (1987). *History of police psychological services*. Washington, DC: Federal Bureau of Investigation.

Reese, J. T., Horn, J. M., & Dunning, C. (1990). *Critical incidents in policing*. Washington, DC: Federal Bureau of Investigation.

Reiser, M. (1974). Some organization stresses on policemen. *Journal of Police Science and Administration, 2*, 156–159.

Robinson, R. C., & Mitchell, J. T. (1995). Getting some balance back into the debriefing debate. *Bulletin of the Australian Psychological Society, 17*, 5–10.

Rogers, C. R. (1961). *On becoming a person: A therapist's view of psychotherapy*. Boston: Houghton Mifflin.

Sack, K., & Elder, J. (2000, July 11). Poll finds optimistic outlook but enduring racial divide. *New York Times*, A1, A23.

Schroedel, J. R., Frisch, S., Hallamore, N., Peterson, J., & Vanderhorst, N. (1996). The joint impact of race and gender on police department employment practices. *Women and Criminal Justice, 8*(2), 59–77.

Schulz, D. M. (1995). *From social worker to crimefighter: Women in United States municipal policing*. Westport, CT: Praeger.

Segrave, K. (1995). *Policewomen: A history*. Jefferson, NC: McFarland.

Selye, H. (1978). The stress of police work. *Police Stress, 1*, 7–8.

Sherman, l. J. (1975). Evaluating policewomen on patrol in a suburban police department. *Journal of Police Science and Administration, 3,* 434–438.

Somodeville, S. A. (1978). The psychologist's role in a police department. *Police Chief, 45,* 21–23.

Souryal, S. S. (1981). The Kojack syndrome: Meeting the problem of police dissatisfaction through job enrichment. *Police Chief, 48,* 60–64.

Stack, S., & Kelley, T. (1994). Police suicide: An analysis. *American Journal of Police, 13,* 73–90.

Sterngold, J. (2000, November 17). Panel rebukes police leaders in Los Angeles. *New York Times,* A17.

Terry, W. (1981). Police stress: The empirical evidence. *Journal of Police Science and Administration, 9,* 61–75.

Toch, H. (1995). Research and reform in community policing. *American Journal of Police, 14,* 1–10.

Toch, H., & Grant, J. D. (1991). *Police as problem solvers.* New York: Plenum.

Toch, H., Grant, J. D., & Galvin, R. T. (1975). *Agents of change: A study in police reform.* Cambridge, MA: Schenkman.

Violanti, J. M., Vena, J. E., & Petralia, S. (1998). Mortality of a police cohort: 1950–1990. *American Journal of Industrial Medicine, 33,* 366–373.

Walker, S. (1992). *The police in America: An introduction.* New York: McGraw-Hill.

Weisburd, G., Greenspan, R., Hamilton, E. E., & Williams, H. (2000). *Police attitudes toward abuse of authority: Findings from a national survey* (Research in Brief). Washington, DC: National Institute of Justice.

Wertsch, T. L. (1998). Walking the thin blue line: Policewomen and tokenism today. *Women and Criminal Justice, 9*(3), 23–61.

Wexler, J. G. (1985). Role styles of women police officers. *Sex Roles, 12,* 749–755.

Worden, A. P. (1993). The attitudes of women and men in policing: Testing conventional and contemporary wisdom. *Criminology, 3,* 203–237.

Wycoff, M. A., & Skogan, W. K. (1993). *Community policing in Madison: Quality from inside out: An evaluation of implementation and impact.* Washington, DC: National Institute of Justice.

Zhao, J., Thuman, Q., & He, N. (1999). Sources of job satisfaction among police officers: A test of demographic and work environment models. *Justice Quarterly, 16,* 153–170.

Appendix A

Letter to Officers

September 22, 1997

Dear Officer:

I am writing to ask you to participate in a study that is examining the stress involved in being a police officer and how this stress affects not only you, but your family as well. Stress has been defined as feelings of emotional strain, pressure, discomfort, anger, uneasiness, and/or tension. Although a great deal of information has been discovered about the effects of stress on police officers (e.g., high rates of heart disease, divorce, serious back problems, etc.), little is understood about the causes of this stress and how it affects officers and their families.

Realizing this, the National Institute of Justice decided to fund research in this area. The Police Department received the only grant offered during Fiscal Year 1997 to study this underdeveloped and very important topic. I believe that the Police Department is the perfect place to study such a difficult topic because both the Police Administration and the Patrolmen's Benevolent Association (PBA) realize the importance of this study and support this effort. Both parties have agreed that this study is a great opportunity to help the department, its officers, and their families better understand

and cope with the stressors that impact the law enforcement community.

It is hoped that this research can help in several fundamental areas:

a) To better understand the sources of stress common to officers of this department.

b) As perhaps you are aware, the Employee Assistance Program (EAP) provides confidential assistance for personal and/or work-related problems faced by officers. This program is distinct from any departmental drug-testing program. The current study seeks to identify areas that can be improved to strengthen the department's Employee Assistance Program (EAP).

c) To identify what can be done to improve officer and supervisor training within the department that will reduce the amount of stress faced by all officers.

d) To better understand the relationship between being employed as a police officer and how this career impacts the officer's family life. It is further hoped that some actions can be taken that will help officers cope with the stress associated with balancing one's family life with one's career.

e) Finally, the National Institute of Justice hopes that what is learned from this department may be helpful to officers—and their families—across the nation.

A great deal of work has been completed by a group of police officers to develop a survey that can be used to help officers of this department (and others) in practical ways. With this in mind, it is very important that you take the time to complete this survey. Please follow the directions provided (if you need additional space to complete the "fill-in" questions, please clearly mark "ON BACK" in the space provided and finish your response on the back of the page). Once you have completed your survey, please place it into the supplied envelope, personally seal the envelope, and give it back to the person who gave it to you (e.g., your lieutenant). All envelopes will be mailed to me through departmental mail. BE SURE NOT TO PUT YOUR NAME ANYWHERE ON THE SURVEY.

Once again, the Administration, the PBA, and I thank you for participating in this important study.

Appendix B

Questionnaire

QUESTIONS

1. Would you say that you are experiencing some work-related discomfort or stress?

    (Please circle the most appropriate response)

    A GREAT DEAL / SOME / VERY LITTLE / NONE

2. Which of the following areas are—or have been—sources of stress for you?

    (Please respond to *both* columns by using the following scale:

    1 = VERY STRESSFUL; 2 = STRESSFUL;
    3 = NOT STRESSFUL).

	Now	In the Past
Inadequate reward or recognition		
Discrimination		
Quality of immediate supervision		
Internal departmental politics		
External political influence		
Inadequate information		
Racial tension in the Department		
The impact of the job on my family		
The Department's leadership		
Problems in the community		
My assignment		

continues on next page

	Now	In the Past
Experiencing violence	_____	_____
Witnessing child abuse	_____	_____
Other (please specify)	_____	_____

_____

_____

_____

3. Do you ever experience unwanted pressures or attention off the job due to your profession?

   OFTEN / SOMETIMES / VERY OCCASIONALLY / NEVER

4. Does your family ever experience unwanted pressures or attention due to your being a police officer?

   OFTEN / SOMETIMES / VERY OCCASIONALLY / NEVER

5. Do you feel that family-related stress has at some juncture affected your work motivation or performance?

   OFTEN / SOMETIMES / VERY OCCASIONALLY / NEVER

6. Do you feel that work-related stress has ever affected your family life or home life?

   OFTEN / SOMETIMES / VERY OCCASIONALLY / NEVER

7. Have you experienced difficulties balancing job and family responsibilities?

   OFTEN / SOMETIMES / VERY OCCASIONALLY / NEVER

8a. Would you say that you are currently experiencing stress as a result of family-related problems?

   A GREAT DEAL / SOME / VERY LITTLE / NONE

b. Please briefly identify or describe the problem. _____

_____

_____

9a. To what extent would additional access to child care/day care facilities for your children relieve stress on your job?

A GREAT DEAL / SOME / VERY LITTLE / NONE

b. If applicable, would you utilize this service?   **YES / NO**

10a. Do you think that your level of motivation or commitment has been diminished by any actions of the Department's administration?

OFTEN / SOMETIMES / VERY OCCASIONALLY / NEVER

b. Please *briefly* specify the actions that have (at some juncture) diminished your enthusiasm for your work. _____

_____

_____

11a. Do you think that your level of motivation or commitment has been diminished by any other aspect(s) of the job?

OFTEN / SOMETIMES / VERY OCCASIONALLY / NEVER

b. Please briefly specify the actions that have diminished your enthusiasm for your work. _____

_____

_____

12. Do you think that at any time your level of motivation or commitment has been adversely affected by experiences of stress?

A GREAT DEAL / SOME / VERY LITTLE / NONE

13. What, if anything, do you do when you feel tense or stressed?
(Please check [✔] when applicable)

Exercise   _____
Church or pray   _____
Music   _____
Activity or hobby   _____
Driving   _____
Social activity   _____
Sleep   _____
Sharing the problem with someone else   _____
Drink alcohol   _____
Use drugs other than alcohol   _____
Medication   _____
Other   _____

_____

_____

14. With whom do you usually discuss work-related concerns or
problems when you have them?
(Please check [✔] when applicable)

Spouse/Significant other _____
Supervisor   _____
Partner   _____
Other officer   _____
Friend   _____
Child   _____ Age of child ___
Physician   _____
No one   _____
Other (please specify)   _____

_____

_____

15. Have you ever found yourself using alcohol to relieve work-
related tension or stress?

OFTEN / SOMETIMES / VERY OCCASIONALLY / NEVER

16. Have you ever experienced nightmares or painful memories related to stressful work experiences?

OFTEN / SOMETIMES / VERY OCCASIONALLY / NEVER

17a. Would you say that you are *currently* experiencing stress as a result of work-related problems?

A GREAT DEAL / SOME / VERY LITTLE / NONE

b. Could you briefly identify the problems? _____

_____

_____

18a. Would you say that you *have ever* experienced serious stress as a result of work-related problems?

OFTEN / SOMETIMES / VERY OCCASIONALLY / NEVER

b. Could you identify the time period and briefly identify the problems? _____

_____

_____

_____

19a. Do you see any problems of fairness in the system for promotions within the Department?

A GREAT DEAL / SOME / VERY LITTLE / NONE

b. Do you feel that your career has been adversely affected by the problems?

A GREAT DEAL / SOME / VERY LITTLE / NONE

20. Do you see media coverage of the Department to be disruptive to your work?

**VERY DISRUPTIVE / DISRUPTIVE /
MAKES NO DIFFERENCE**

21a. How much of a role do you think that external forces (e.g., political groups, business groups, community groups, etc.) play in influencing Departmental policy?

A GREAT DEAL / SOME / VERY LITTLE / NONE

b. Do you think that these external forces should have more influence or less influence on Departmental policy?

MORE INFLUENCE / LESS INFLUENCE

22. Do you feel that your career opportunities have been adversely affected by political considerations or political pressures?

A GREAT DEAL / SOME / VERY LITTLE / NONE

23. To what extent do you think that external political pressures adversely affect the Department's effectiveness?

A GREAT DEAL / SOME / VERY LITTLE / NONE

24. How would you characterize, in one sentence, or two, the current status of racial relations in the Department? _____

_____
_____
_____

25a. Are you personally concerned about issues of fairness in the Department related to race or gender?

GREATLY CONCERNED / SOMEWHAT CONCERNED / NOT AT ALL CONCERNED

b. Please describe any unfairness you perceive that concerns you. _____

_____
_____

26a. Do you feel that you personally have experienced racial or gender discrimination at work?

A GREAT DEAL / SOME / VERY LITTLE / NONE

b. Please very briefly describe the unfairness you perceive that concerns you _____

_____

_____

27a. Do you feel that you personally have experienced racial or gender discrimination at work?

OFTEN / SOMETIMES / VERY OCCASIONALLY / NEVER

b. *IF YOU DO*, what was the source of the discrimination?
(Please check [✔] when applicable)

Administration   _____
Supervisors   _____
Fellow officers or partners   _____
Members of the public   _____
Other (please specify)   _____

_____

_____

28. Do you feel the Department's climate relative to race relations adversely affects your motivation or performance?

A GREAT DEAL / SOME / VERY LITTLE / NONE

29. Do you feel that enough attention has been given to the issues of race and gender in the Department?

**NOT ENOUGH ATTENTION / ENOUGH ATTENTION /
TOO MUCH ATTENTION**

30. What, if any, issues relating to race or gender do you feel require additional attention? _____

_____

_____

31. Do you have any preferences as to who you have as a riding partner that relate to race or to gender?

a. race   **YES / NO**
b. gender   **YES / NO**

32. Do you feel more comfortable or less comfortable when you work with someone of a different race?

   **MORE COMFORTABLE / LESS COMFORTABLE /
   MAKES NO DIFFERENCE**

33. Do you feel more comfortable or less comfortable when you work with someone of the opposite sex?

   **MORE COMFORTABLE / LESS COMFORTABLE /
   MAKES NO DIFFERENCE**

34. Do you feel that racial considerations place constraints on your opportunity to advance in the Department?

   A GREAT DEAL / SOME / VERY LITTLE / NONE

35. Do you feel that gender considerations place constraints on your opportunity to advance in your profession?

   A GREAT DEAL / SOME / VERY LITTLE / NONE

36. Have you found your immediate supervisors in the Department to be largely helpful and supportive, or unhelpful and unsupportive?

   (Please check [✔] when applicable)

   HELPFUL   _____
   SUPPORTIVE   _____
   UNHELPFUL   _____
   UNSUPPORTIVE   _____

37. To what extent have you felt that your immediate supervisors have treated you fairly?

   **ALWAYS FAIRLY / MOSTLY FAIRLY /
   SOMETIMES UNFAIRLY / MOSTLY UNFAIRLY**

38. To what degree has fairness of supervision become an issue that affects how you feel about your work?

   A GREAT DEAL / SOME / VERY LITTLE / NONE

39. Do you feel you have a sufficient understanding for what the top brass of this Department defines as its mission?

A STRONG UNDERSTANDING / SOME UNDERSTANDING / NOT SURE / HAVE NO IDEA

40. Do you have any suggestions as to what the Department could do to assist officers by improving any aspect(s) of officer or supervisor training? _____

_____

_____

41a. Do you feel you receive an adequate amount of information to properly do your job?

MORE THAN ENOUGH / ADEQUATE / LESS THAN ADEQUATE / NOT NEARLY ENOUGH

b. What sort of additional information do you feel would help you to better do your job? _____

_____

_____

42a. Have you ever felt that inadequate information has endangered your physical safety?

OFTEN / SOMETIMES / VERY OCCASIONALLY / NEVER

b. Please briefly describe any perceived problem. _____

_____

_____

43. Are you aware of the Employee Assistance Program (EAP) available in this department?

YES / NO

44. Have you ever used the EAP program, or do you know anyone who has ever used the program?

HAVE USED / KNOW SOMEONE WHO HAS USED / NO

45. Do you personally have confidence or trust in the EAP program?

   A GREAT DEAL / SOME / VERY LITTLE / NONE

46. Is there anything you can suggest that would improve the Department's EAP program or otherwise assist officers with work-related problems related to stress? _____

   _____

   _____

   _____

   _____

   _____

Age _____   Ethnicity   Gender
             _____ African American   (check one)
             _____ Caucasian/White   _____ Male
             _____ Mexican American/Hispanic _____ Female
             _____ Native American
             _____ Other

Marital Status (check one)

_____ Single
_____ Married
_____ Divorced
_____ Widowed
_____ Other (please specify)

Please check the highest level of schooling you have completed:

_____ High school graduate   _____ Some college
                                        (degree not completed)
_____ Associate degree   _____ Bachelor degree
_____ Graduate degree   _____ Other (please specify)

What is your current rank? (check one)

_____ Police officer   _____ First line supervisor
_____ Detective   _____ Captain or above

What is your current assigment?

      Administration / Investigation / Traffic Patrol

How many years have you been employed by this department?

_____ Years

Do you have a second job?   YES / NO

Appendix C

Responses to Questionnaire

		Response %	
Question	Code	City	Suburban
1. Would you say that you are experiencing some work-related discomfort or stress?	A. A great deal	15.6	9.6
	B. Some	44.2	56.7
	C. Very little	20.1	19.2
	D. None	4.8	6.7
	I. No response	15.2	7.7

Which of the following areas are—or have been—sources of stress for you?

Question	Code	City	Suburban
2. Inadequate reward or recognition (now)	A. Very stressful	13.4	9.6
	B. Stressful	29.7	29.8
	C. Not stressful	46.8	54.8
	I. No response	10.0	5.8
3. Inadequate reward or recognition (in the past)	A. Very stressful	16.7	18.3
	B. Stressful	33.8	26.9
	C. Not stressful	33.5	48.1
	I. No response	16.0	6.7
4. Discrimination (now)	A. Very stressful	14.1	5.8
	B. Stressful	26.8	15.4
	C. Not stressful	46.1	75.0
	I. No response	13.0	3.8

Question	Code	Response %	
		City	Suburban
5. Discrimination (in the past)	A. Very stressful	15.6	7.7
	B. Stressful	24.5	10.6
	C. Not stressful	37.9	73.1
	I. No response	21.9	8.7
6. Quality of immediate supervision (now)	A. Very stressful	12.3	16.3
	B. Stressful	23.8	28.8
	C. Not stressful	44.2	52.9
	I. No response	19.7	1.9
7. Quality of immediate supervision (in the past)	A. Very stressful	22.7	19.2
	B. Stressful	25.3	40.4
	C. Not stressful	28.6	35.6
	I. No response	23.4	4.8
8. Internal departmental politics (now)	A. Very stressful	34.9	40.4
	B. Stressful	35.3	43.3
	C. Not stressful	15.6	14.4
	I. No response	14.1	1.9
9. Internal departmental politics (in the past)	A. Very stressful	34.9	38.5
	B. Stressful	30.5	39.4
	C. Not stressful	16.4	17.3
	I. No response	18.2	4.8
10. External political influences (now)	A. Very stressful	30.1	18.3
	B. Stressful	27.9	26.0
	C. Not stressful	32.7	51.9
	I. No response	9.3	3.8
11. External political influences (in the past)	A. Very stressful	25.7	18.3
	B. Stressful	29.4	31.7
	C. Not stressful	30.1	45.2
	I. No response	14.9	4.8
12. Inadequate information (now)	A. Very stressful	31.2	23.1
	B. Stressful	39.4	46.2
	C. Not stressful	20.4	28.8
	I. No response	8.9	1.9

Question	Code	Response %	
		City	Suburban
13. Inadequate information (in the past)	A. Very stressful	24.5	18.3
	B. Stressful	36.8	49.0
	C. Not stressful	20.1	26.9
	I. No response	18.6	5.6
14. Racial tension in the Department (now)	A. Very stressful	16.4	—
	B. Stressful	34.6	—
	C. Not stressful	36.8	—
	I. No response	12.3	—
15. Racial tension in the Department (in the past)	A. Very stressful	14.5	—
	B. Stressful	27.9	—
	C. Not stressful	36.4	—
	I. No response	21.2	—
16. The impact of the job on my family (now)	A. Very stressful	10.0	3.8
	B. Stressful	31.2	46.2
	C. Not stressful	34.6	47.1
	I. No response	24.2	2.9
17. The impact of the job on my family (in the past)	A. Very stressful	11.5	8.7
	B. Stressful	26.8	43.3
	C. Not stressful	33.8	44.2
	I. No response	27.9	3.8
18. The Department's leadership (now)	A. Very stressful	35.3	49.0
	B. Stressful	30.9	36.5
	C. Not stressful	19.3	12.5
	I. No response	14.5	1.9
19. The Department's leadership (in the past)	A. Very stressful	26.4	31.7
	B. Stressful	29.4	43.3
	C. Not stressful	24.2	20.2
	I. No response	20.1	4.8
20. Problems in the community (now)	A. Very stressful	14.5	1.9
	B. Stressful	43.1	35.6
	C. Not stressful	30.5	60.6
	I. No response	11.5	1.9

Question	Code	Response % City	Suburban
21. Problems in the community (in the past)	A. Very stressful	11.2	1.9
	B. Stressful	40.1	31.7
	C. Not stressful	34.6	61.5
	I. No response	14.1	4.8
22. My assignment (now)	A. Very stressful	7.4	5.8
	B. Stressful	30.1	37.5
	C. Not stressful	50.2	54.8
	I. No response	12.3	1.9
23. My assignment (in the past)	A. Very stressful	10.4	5.8
	B. Stressful	29.7	32.7
	C. Not stressful	39.8	56.7
	I. No response	20.1	4.8
24. Experiencing violence (now)	A. Very stressful	8.2	2.9
	B. Stressful	34.9	31.7
	C. Not stressful	43.9	63.5
	I. No response	13.0	1.9
25. Experiencing violence (in the past)	A. Very stressful	11.5	3.8
	B. Stressful	33.5	34.7
	C. Not stressful	35.7	56.7
	I. No response	19.3	4.8
26. Witnessing child abuse (now)	A. Very stressful	26.0	26.0
	B. Stressful	36.1	34.5
	C. Not stressful	17.8	37.5
	I. No response	20.1	1.9
27. Witnessing child abuse (in the past)	A. Very stressful	28.3	26.9
	B. Stressful	29.7	32.7
	C. Not stressful	20.8	36.5
	I. No response	21.2	3.8
28. Other (open-ended question)	A. Did not reply	88.5	92.3
	B. Replied	11.5	7.7
29. Do you ever experience unwanted pressures or attention off the job due to your profession?	A. Often	17.8	13.5
	B. Sometimes	49.1	58.7
	C. Very occasionally	19.3	24.0
	D. Never	8.6	3.8
	I. No response	5.2	0.0

Question	Code	Response % City	Suburban
30. Does your family ever experience unwanted pressures or attention due to your being a police officer?	A. Often	7.4	6.7
	B. Sometimes	41.6	42.3
	C. Very occasionally	24.9	32.7
	D. Never	20.4	18.3
	I. No response	5.6	0.0
31. Do you feel that family-related stress has at some juncture affected your work motivation or performance?	A. Often	9.3	1.0
	B. Sometimes	37.5	42.3
	C. Very occasionally	27.1	34.6
	D. Never	22.3	22.1
	I. No response	3.7	0.0
32. Do you feel that work-related stress has ever affected your family life or home life?	A. Often	16.7	9.6
	B. Sometimes	49.4	53.8
	C. Very occasionally	19.3	30.8
	D. Never	12.3	5.8
	I. No response	2.2	0.0
33. Have you experienced difficulties balancing job and family responsibilities?	A. Often	10.0	2.9
	B. Sometimes	36.1	38.5
	C. Very occasionally	26.0	28.8
	D. Never	24.9	29.8
	I. No response	2.6	0.0
34. Would you say that you are currently experiencing stress as a result of family-related problems?	A. A great deal	9.3	4.8
	B. Some	27.1	23.1
	C. Very little	28.6	31.7
	D. None	28.3	40.4
	I. No response	6.7	0.0

Please briefly identify or describe the problem.

Question	Code	City	Suburban
35. To what extent would additional access to child care/day care facilities for your children relieve stress on your job?	A. A great deal	19.0	6.7
	B. Some	12.6	16.3
	C. Very little	8.2	8.7
	D. None	51.7	64.4
	I. No response	8.6	3.8
36. If applicable, would you utilize this service?	A. No	29.4	39.4
	B. Yes	42.8	29.8
	I. No response	27.8	30.8

		Response %	
Question	Code	City	Suburban

		Response %	
Question	Code	City	Suburban
37. Do you think that your level of motivation or commitment has been diminished by any actions of the Department's administration?	A. Often	39.8	49.0
	B. Sometimes	30.9	31.7
	C. Very occasionally	15.6	12.5
	D. Never	6.7	6.7
	I. No response	7.1	0.0

Please *briefly* specify the actions that have (at some juncture) diminished your enthusiasm for your work.

38. Do you think that your level of motivation or commitment has been diminished by any other aspect(s) of the job?	A. Often	22.3	7.7
	B. Sometimes	34.6	45.2
	C. Very occasionally	19.3	25.0
	D. Never	13.4	21.2
	I. No response	10.4	1.0

Please briefly specify the actions that have diminished your enthusiasm for your work.

39. Do you think that at any time your level of motivation or commitment has been adversely affected by experiences of stress?	A. A great deal	17.5	9.6
	B. Some	40.9	46.2
	C. Very little	23.4	30.8
	D. None	9.7	11.5
	I. No response	8.6	1.9

What, if anything, do you do when you feel tense or stressed?

40. Exercise	A. No	34.6	31.7
	B. Yes	58.7	67.3
	C. No response	6.3	1.0
41. Church or pray	A. No	55.8	81.7
	B. Yes	41.3	18.3
	C. No response	3.0	0.0
42. Music	A. No	49.4	52.9
	B. Yes	48.0	47.1
	C. No response	2.6	0.0

Question	Code	Response % City	Response % Suburban
43. Activity or hobby	A. No	47.2	30.8
	B. Yes	44.6	69.2
	C. No response	8.2	0.0
44. Driving	A. No	70.6	76.0
	B. Yes	22.7	24.0
	C. No response	6.7	0.0
45. Social activity	A. No	58.7	72.1
	B. Yes	32.7	27.9
	C. No response	8.6	0.0
46. Sleep	A. No	45.4	54.8
	B. Yes	46.8	45.2
	C. No response	7.8	0.0
47. Sharing the problem with someone else	A. No	47.2	55.8
	B. Yes	44.6	44.2
	C. No response	8.2	0.0
48. Drink alcohol	A. No	49.4	75.0
	B. Yes	39.0	25.0
	C. No response	11.5	0.0
49. Use drugs other than alcohol	A. No	87.4	98.1
	B. Yes	1.5	1.9
	C. No response	11.2	0.0
50. Medication	A. No	88.8	94.2
	B. Yes	5.6	5.8
	C. No response	5.6	0.0
Other	Not Coded		

With whom do you usually discuss work-related concerns or problems when you have them?

51. Spouse/Significant other	A. No	34.6	34.6
	B. Yes	61.3	65.4
	C. No response	4.1	0.0

		Response %	
Question	Code	City	Suburban
52. Supervisor	A. No	80.3	82.7
	B. Yes	17.8	17.3
	C. No response	1.9	0.0
53. Partner	A. No	37.9	55.8
	B. Yes	55.4	44.2
	C. No response	6.7	0.0
54. Other officer	A. No	44.6	51.0
	B. Yes	48.7	49.0
	C. No response	6.7	0.0
55. Friend	A. No	47.6	58.7
	B. Yes	45.0	41.3
	C. No response	7.4	0.0
56. Child	A. No	88.5	98.1
	B. Yes	3.3	1.9
	C. No response	8.2	0.0
57. Physician	A. No	88.8	96.2
	B. Yes	2.6	3.8
	C. No response	8.6	0.0
58. No one	A. No	80.3	87.5
	B. Yes	10.0	12.5
	C. No response	9.7	0.0
59. Other (open-ended question)	A. No reply	93.7	93.3
	B. Reply	6.3	6.7
60. Have you ever found yourself using alcohol to relieve work-related tension or stress?	A. Often	10.8	1.9
	B. Sometimes	29.4	20.2
	C. Very occasionally	20.8	24.0
	D. Never	34.9	53.8
	I. No response	4.1	0.0
61. Have you ever experienced nightmares or painful memories related to stressful work experiences?	A. Often	8.6	1.0
	B. Sometimes	26.8	17.3
	C. Very occasionally	24.9	26.9
	D. Never	30.5	54.8
	I. No response	9.3	0.0

Question	Code	Response %	
		City	Suburban
62. Would you say that you are *currently* experiencing stress as a result of work-related problems?	A. A great deal	12.3	9.6
	B. Some	29.4	30.8
	C. Very little	28.6	26.0
	D. None	24.5	33.7
	I. No response	5.2	0.0

Could you briefly identify the problems?

Question	Code	Response %	
63. Would you say that you *have ever* experienced serious stress as a result of work-related problems?	A. Often	13.0	4.8
	B. Sometimes	33.1	31.7
	C. Very occasionally	23.8	31.7
	D. Never	22.7	31.7
	I. No response	7.4	0.0

Could you identify the time period and briefly identify the problems?

Question	Code	Response %	
64. Do you see any problems of fairness in the system for promotions within the Department?	A. A great deal	40.9	43.3
	B. Some	29.7	38.5
	C. Very little	11.2	13.5
	D. None	10.4	4.8
	I. No response	7.8	0.0
65. Do you feel that your career has been adversely affected by the problems?	A. A great deal	17.8	19.2
	B. Some	29.0	28.8
	C. Very little	20.8	29.8
	D. None	21.9	22.1
	I. No response	10.4	0.0
66. Do you see media coverage of the Department to be disruptive to your work?	A. Very disruptive	30.9	3.8
	B. Disruptive	36.8	26.9
	C. Makes no difference	19.0	68.3
	I. No response	13.3	0.0
67. How much of a role do you think that external forces play in influencing Departmental policy?	A. A great deal	50.6	44.2
	B. Some	30.9	46.2
	C. Very little	3.0	8.7
	D. None	2.2	1.0
	I. No response	13.4	0.0

		Response %	
Question	Code	City	Suburban

68. Do you think that these external forces should have more influence or less influence on Departmental policy?	A. More influence B. Less influence I. No response	6.3 79.2 14.5	5.8 90.4 3.8
69. Do you feel that your career opportunities have been adversely affected by political considerations or political pressures?	A. A great deal B. Some C. Very little D. None I. No response	26.4 31.2 15.2 19.3 7.8	12.5 24.0 33.7 28.8 1.0
70. To what extent do you think that external political pressures adversely affect the Department's effectiveness?	A. A great deal B. Some C. Very little D. None I. No response	46.1 37.5 6.7 2.2 7.4	37.5 46.2 12.5 2.9 1.0

How would you characterize, in one sentence, or two, the current status of racial relations in the Department?

71. Are you personally concerned about issues of fairness in the Department related to race or gender?	A. Greatly concerned B. Somewhat concerned C. Not at all concerned I. No response	33.1 37.2 21.6 8.1	4.8 25.0 69.2 1.0

Please describe any unfairness you perceive that concerns you.

72. Do you feel that you personally have experienced racial or gender discrimination at work?	A. A great deal B. Some C. Very little D. None I. No response	12.6 30.5 18.2 32.0 6.7	3.8 6.7 10.6 78.8 0.0

Please very briefly describe the unfairness you perceive that concerns you.

Question	Code	Response %	
		City	Suburban
73. Do you feel that you personally have experienced racial or gender discrimination at work?	A. Often	10.4	2.9
	B. Sometimes	32.7	6.7
	C. Very occasionally	17.8	11.5
	D. Never	29.4	76.9
	I. No response	9.7	1.9

IF YOU DO, what was the source of the discrimination?

Question	Code	City	Suburban
74. Administration	A. No	58.0	85.6
	B. Yes	32.3	14.4
	C. No response	9.7	0.0
75. Supervisors	A. No	58.4	89.4
	B. Yes	26.0	9.6
	C. No response	15.6	1.0
76. Fellow officers or partners	A. No	50.6	96.2
	B. Yes	29.7	3.8
	C. No response	19.7	0.0
77. Members of the public	A. No	46.1	96.2
	B. Yes	34.9	3.8
	C. No response	19.0	0.0
78. Other (open-ended question)	A. Did not reply	95.5	99.0
	B. Replied	4.5	1.0
79. Do you feel the Department's climate relative to race relations adversely affects your motivation or performance?	A. A great deal	14.9	2.9
	B. Some	26.8	10.6
	C. Very little	23.8	19.2
	D. None	27.9	67.3
	I. No response	6.7	0.0
80. Do you feel that enough attention has been given to the issues of race and gender in the Department?	A. Not enough attention	33.1	8.7
	B. Enough attention	30.9	63.5
	C. Too much attention	20.4	25.0
	I. No response	15.6	2.9

What, if any, issues relating to race or gender do you feel require additional attention?

		Response %	
Question	Code	City	Suburban
81. Do you have any preference as to who you have as a riding partner that relate to race?	A. No B. Yes I. No response	73.6 16.0 10.4	— — —
82. Do you have any preference as to who you have as a riding partner that relate to gender?	A. No B. Yes I. No response	63.6 30.9 5.6	70.2 27.9 1.9
83. Do you feel more comfortable or less comfortable when you work with someone of a different race?	A. More comfortable B. Less comfortable C. No difference I. No response	0.4 20.4 74.7 4.5	— — — —
84. Do you feel more comfortable or less comfortable when you work with someone of the opposite sex?	A. More comfortable B. Less comfortable C. No difference I. No response	1.9 34.9 58.4 4.9	1.0 33.7 62.5 2.9
85. Do you feel that racial considerations place constraints on your opportunity to advance in the Department?	A. A great deal B. Some C. Very little D. None I. No response	16.0 32.0 18.2 27.1 6.7	— — — — —
86. Do you feel that gender considerations place constraints on your opportunity to advance in the Department?	A. A great deal B. Some C. Very little D. None I. No response	11.2 29.7 23.4 30.5 5.2	4.8 18.3 26.0 50.0 1.0
87. To what extent have you felt that your immediate supervisors have treated you fairly?	A. Always fairly B. Mostly fairly C. Sometimes unfairly D. Mostly unfairly I. No response	21.6 48.7 17.5 4.8 7.5	9.6 62.5 21.2 6.7 0.0

| | | Response % | |
Question	Code	City	Suburban
88. To what degree has fairness of supervision become an issue that affects how you feel about your work?	A. A great deal B. Some C. Very little D. None I. No response	29.0 33.1 25.3 9.3 3.3	28.8 32.7 26.9 11.5 0.0
89. Do you feel you have a sufficient understanding for what the top brass of this Department defines as its mission?	A. A strong understanding B. Some understanding C. Not sure D. Have no idea I. No response	10.8 29.0 22.3 34.6 3.3	6.7 28.8 24.0 37.5 2.9

Do you have any suggestions as to what the Department could do to assist officers by improving any aspect(s) of officer or supervisor training?

Question	Code	City	Suburban
90. Do you feel you receive an adequate amount of information to properly do your job?	A. More than enough B. Adequate C. Less than adequate D. Not nearly enough I. No response	1.9 36.4 30.1 22.3 9.3	4.8 58.7 28.8 7.7 0.0

What sort of additional information do you feel would help you to better do your job?

Question	Code	City	Suburban
91. Have you ever felt that inadequate information has endangered your physical safety?	A. Often B. Sometimes C. Very occasionally D. Never I. No response	13.4 43.5 16.7 12.6 13.8	3.8 41.3 38.5 14.4 1.9

Please briefly describe any perceived problem.

Question	Code	City	Suburban
92. Are you aware of the EAP available in this department?	A. No B. Yes I. No response	7.4 75.5 17.1	17.3 81.7 1.0

Question	Code	Response %	
		City	Suburban
93. Have you ever used the Employee Assistance Program (EAP) program, or do you know anyone who has ever used the program?	A. Have used	10.0	6.7
	B. Know someone who has used	25.3	17.3
	C. No	40.1	58.7
	I. No response	24.5	17.3
94. Do you personally have confidence or trust in the EAP program?	A. A great deal	11.9	2.9
	B. Some	38.3	33.6
	C. Very little	14.1	26.0
	D. None	16.4	26.0
	I. No response	19.3	11.5

Is there anything you can suggest that would improve the department's EAP program or otherwise assist officers with work-related problems related to stress?

Question	Code	No. of responses	
95. Age	A. 18–23 years	1	0
	B. 24–28 years	20	3
	C. 29–33 years	40	9
	D. 34–38 years	59	21
	E. 39–43 years	54	14
	F. 44–48 years	26	15
	G. 49–53 years	14	13
	H. 54–58 years	9	7
	I. No response	44	21
	J. 59+ years	2	1
96. Ethnicity	A. African American	39	1
	B. Caucasian/White	163	95
	C. Mexican American/ Hispanic	12	0
	D. Native American	1	0
	E. Other	5	0
	I. No response	49	8
97. Gender	A. Male	166	89
	B. Female	45	3
	I. No response	58	12

			No. of responses	
98. Marital status	A.	Single	43	14
	B.	Married	148	79
	C.	Divorced	27	5
	D.	Widow	2	0
	E.	Other	6	2
	I.	No response	43	4
99. Education	A.	High school graduate	29	7
	B.	Some college (degree not completed)	89	18
	C.	Associate degree	42	35
	D.	Bachelor degree	66	35
	E.	Graduate degree	5	2
	F.	Other	2	2
	I.	No response	36	5
100. Current rank	A.	Police officer	173	65
	B.	First line supervisor	38	18
	C.	Detective	29	12
	D.	Captain or above	14	1
101. Current assignment	A.	Administration	13	9
	B.	Investigation	30	15
	C.	Traffic/patrol	192	67
	I.	No response	34	13
102. Years employed by department	A.	1–5 years	55	8
	B.	6–10 years	37	24
	C.	11–15 years	65	13
	D.	16–20 years	34	25
	E.	21–25 years	14	16
	F.	26–30 years	23	6
	G.	31–35 years	8	2
	H.	36–40 years	0	0
	I.	No response	33	10
	J.	41+ years	0	0
103. Do you have a second job?	A.	No	160	62
	B.	Yes	83	35
	I.	No response	26	7

Fractions of 1% can be considered rounding errors.

Index

Action research
  benefits of, 12–13
  collaborative research link, 17
  division of labor in, 129
  survey implications for, 146–149
Actualization, 151–171
  administrative resistance to, 172–177
  definition, 151–152
  interview excerpts, 153–172
  and problem-oriented policing, 151–153
Acute stress, 5
Administration-related stress. *See also* "Politics"
  and authoritarian practices, 89–90
  centralized, top-down management link, 198–199
  city and suburban sample, 87, 139–140
  data feedback sessions, 131–133, 138–142
  focus group results, 74–76
  and innovation resistance, 172–177
  interview descriptions of, 47–49
  participatory management in, 203–205
  and patriarch family analogy, 89–90
  reform suggestions, 203–206
  research overview, 88–89
  and specialist officers, 172–177
  suburban sample, 138–142
  survey results, 80–82, 86
  workshop suggestions, 132–133
Affirmative action, 51, 206
African-American officers. *See* Black officers

Age factors
  in family-related stress, 107–109, 112–113, 135, 200
  feedback session results, 135
Alcohol use/abuse
  city versus suburban sample, 87, 135
  focus group reports, 77–78
  interview descriptions, 70
  and lingering work stress, 70
  self-report study limitations, 9–10
Alcoholics Anonymous. *See* Peer counseling
Authoritarian administrative policies, 89–90
Autonomy, 203

Black female officers
  citizen response, 98–99
  "ride-along" field observations, 102–103
  and sexism, 102
  statistical trends, 92n1
Black officers
  "bonding" of, 118–119
  career opportunities perception, 123–124
  community policing view, 125–126
  coping strategies, 118–119
  discrimination against, 119–126, 206–208
    possible solutions, 127–128, 207–208
  divergent perceptions, 206–208
  interview findings, 58–61
  "political" complaints, 100–101
  promotional fairness issue, 118–119
  questionnaire return rate, 15, 15n5

251

About the Author

Hans Toch is distinguished professor at the University at Albany of the State University of New York, where he is affiliated with the School of Criminal Justice. He obtained his PhD in social psychology at Princeton University, has taught at Michigan State University and at Harvard University, and, in 1996, served as Walker-Ames Professor at the University of Washington, Seattle. Dr. Toch is a Fellow of both the American Psychological Association (APA) and the American Society of Criminology. In 1996, he acted as president of the American Association of Correctional Psychology. He is a recipient of the Hadley Cantril Memorial Award and, in 2001, of the August Vollmer Award of the American Society of Criminology for outstanding contributions to applied criminology.

Dr. Toch's research interests range from mental health problems and the psychology of violence to issues of organizational reform and planned change. He has conducted research on prison systems in Michigan, California, New York State, and Scotland and in several police departments across the United States.

Dr. Toch's books include *Police as Problem Solvers* (with J. Douglas Grant, 1991), *Violent Men* (APA, 1992), *Living in Prison* (APA, 1992), *Mosaic of Despair* (APA, 1992), *The Disturbed Violent Offender* (with Kenneth Adams, APA, 1994), *Police Violence* (with William Geller, 1996), *Corrections: A Humanistic Approach* (1997), and *Crime and Punishment* (with Robert Johnson, 2000).